# Working with Groups to Overcome

# Panic Anxiety & Phobias

## Structured Exercises in Healing

# Working with Groups to Overcome

# Panic Anxiety & Phobias

## Structured Exercises in Healing

Shirley Babior, LCSW, MFCC
Carol Goldman, LICSW

WHOLE PERSON ASSOCIATES
Duluth, Minnesota

Library of Congress Catalog Card Number 95-62472
ISBN 1-57025-117-7

WHOLE PERSON ASSOCIATES
210 W Michigan
Duluth MN 55802-1908
800-247-6789

# About the Authors

Shirley Babior, LCSW, MFCC, is a therapist in private practice in San Diego, California, where she is Director of the Center for Anxiety and Stress Treatment. She specializes in treating anxiety disorders, in groups and individually. As a Certified Employee Assistance Professional, Shirley provides services to employees suffering from anxiety and stress in the workplace. She has lectured on the treatment of anxiety disorders at numerous professional meetings and adult education workshops and is the coauthor of two research articles with the University of California at San Diego's Department of Psychiatry. Shirley is a former regional governor of the Phobia Society of America and board member of the Society of Behavioral Medicine. She provides consultation, utilization management, quality improvement, peer review, and assessor/external EAP services to managed care organizations.

Carol Goldman, LICSW, was director of Behavior Associates from 1977 to 1989. She is a founding director of the Boston Institute of Cognitive-Behavior Therapies, a training program for mental health professionals. As the past president of the Greater Boston Phobia Society, Carol is currently in private practice in Boston, Massachusetts. She specializes in cognitive-behavior therapy, family systems, and couples therapy, and provides training to professionals on brief treatment and managed care.

*Overcoming Panic, Anxiety, & Phobias*, the self-help book written by Shirley Babior and Carol Goldman as a companion to this therapist's manual, can be purchased direct from the publisher. Order information is printed on page 180.

# Contents

©1996 Whole Person Press 210 W Michigan Duluth MN 55802     (800) 247-6789

# Introduction

Our era has been called "The Age of Anxiety." As health care providers, we see people on a daily basis who are overwhelmed by the effects of excess anxiety and panic attacks. In fact, panic and other anxiety disorders are more prevalent in the general population than any other mental health problem, including substance abuse.

As a result of anxiety disorders, people's lives may become restricted or filled with worry and tension. Family, friends, and job opportunities can be negatively affected. Scary symptoms can lead desperate people to overuse medical services. People may suffer from more than one type of anxiety disorder, compounding their distress, and their anxiety problems may mask the symptoms of other treatable disorders such as depression and substance abuse.

We wrote this manual as well as our self-help book, *Overcoming Panic, Anxiety, & Phobias*, to provide therapists and their clients with information about and practical tools for treating panic disorder with and without agoraphobia, specific phobias, social phobia, and generalized anxiety disorder. The strategies described in this book are also useful for people experiencing high levels of stress. Too often, people are treated by professionals who are not familiar with the most current treatment regimens for these disorders. Fortunately, cognitive-behavior therapy, upon which our manual is based, has been tested by researchers around the world and found to be effective for treatment of people with anxiety disorders.

The exercises in this book can be used successfully with individuals or groups. We have found it particularly effective, however, to combine the benefits provided by group therapy with a between-session focus on individual goals supported by *Overcoming Panic, Anxiety, & Phobias,* our self-help book. The groups, which are

©1996 Whole Person Press 210 W Michigan Duluth MN 55802      (800) 247-6789

psycho-educational in nature, provide a nonthreatening, supportive environment where participants can learn the cognitive-behavioral strategies needed to manage their anxiety, see that others share
their often secret distress, and gain an arena in which to begin
exposure to their worries and fears. The emphasis is on problem
solving, and out-of-session practice is encouraged. Groups are
time-limited so that participants can gain a sense of accomplishment on their own, but booster sessions can be offered or support
groups formed to help solidify gains.

In this manual, we have included assessment tools, relaxation
scripts, cognitive strategies to challenge overestimates of threat and
catastrophic thinking, and exposure techniques to help people face
their fears. The book also provides support for lifestyle changes,
information for family and friends, and skills for relapse prevention. The exercises in this manual are directly related to specific
pages in *Overcoming Panic, Anxiety, & Phobias,* so clients are able
to prepare themselves for the group activity by reading and practicing at home.

All of the material, in conjunction with the *Overcoming Panic,
Anxiety, & Phobias,* can be adapted for individual sessions, worksite
lectures, all-day seminars, or workshops. The brief exercises can be
combined for one longer presentation.

We have indicated which exercises need to be run by a mental
health professional. Others can be used by nonprofessionals. If you
are using this manual in a support group, bring in mental health
professionals for the exercises that require their expertise.

If you are a therapist, we encourage you, when dealing with specific
anxiety disorders, to use as examples cases from your own practice
(completely disguised, of course). For example, if you are running a
group for clients with specific phobias, it would be helpful to use, as
examples, people who have recovered from a fear of heights, flying,
elevators, insects, etc. You can also use excerpts from the recovery
stories in *Overcoming Panic, Anxiety, & Phobias.*

©1996 Whole Person Press 210 W Michigan Duluth MN 55802      (800) 247-6789

In the last section of this book, we included sample treatment plans and subjective outcomes scales to document your clients' progress. Managed care organizations have changed the way many of us practice. These guidelines, as well as our entire manual, will help you formulate specific diagnoses, design appropriate brief treatment plans, and document treatment progress. In addition, strengthening your skills in running groups for people with anxiety disorders will enhance your ability to market yourself and to get referrals from managed care networks.

We encourage you to supplement your knowledge by reading the articles and books on anxiety disorders listed in our bibliography as well as by attending local, regional, and national meetings on this topic. All nonphysician therapists should develop working relationships with psychopharmacologists, primary care physicians, and specialists such as cardiologists who treat people with anxiety disorders. Coordinated assessment, diagnosis, and treatment is particularly important when treating disorders which affect both the body and the mind.

We hope you find this manual helpful in your work. We have designed it to be used creatively; however, the cognitive-behavioral treatment underpinnings should always be present. We wish you success and welcome all comments.

Shirley Babior, LCSW

Carol Goldman, LICSW

1996

©1996 Whole Person Press 210 W Michigan Duluth MN 55802     (800) 247-6789

# Basic Recovery
# Exercises

## THE FORMAT

The format of *Working with Groups to Overcome Panic, Anxiety, & Phobias* is designed for easy use. You'll find that each exercise is described completely, including: goals, group size, time frame, materials needed, step-by-step process instructions, and variations.

☞ Special instructions for the trainer are preceded by a pointer.

✔ Questions to ask the group are preceded by a check.

➤ Directions for group activities are indicated by an arrow.

▪ Mini-lecture notes are preceded by a bullet.

The activities in this book are not intended as a substitute for medical or psychological counseling. The authors and the publisher disclaim any responsibility or liability resulting from the application of procedures advocated or discussed in this book.

©1996 Whole Person Press 210 W Michigan Duluth MN 55802　　　(800) 247-6789

# My Story

This exercise works very well as an introductory session because it helps set the stage for the work that will be done and because it allows participants in a group to see that they are not alone. Those reluctant to speak in groups are often encouraged to do so when others voice problems similar to, or even worse than, their own problems.

## Goals

To reinforce each participant's sense that real problem-solving is about to occur.

To reduce the stress of the initial meeting.

To allow participants to become used to hearing their concerns voiced aloud.

To build trust in group participants, particularly those with social anxiety, that their concerns will be respected and that they will not be pushed into speaking in the group until they are ready to do so.

## Group Size

Unlimited.

## Time

1–2 hours.

## Materials

Pencils; paper; easel and easel paper; markers.

## Participant Preparation

Pages 1, 2, 21–27 of *Overcoming Panic, Anxiety, & Phobias* will help participants prepare for this session and will reinforce what they learn during the session.

## Process

☞ *This exercise is most appropriate for an ongoing group. If the group has more than ten participants, consider using one of the variations described on page 4.*

1. Introduce the goals of the session.

2. Because feeling safe in the group is crucial to continued participation, reassure participants that they need not speak if they feel uncomfortable doing so. Here are some guidelines:

   ▪ If you wish to remain silent, say I pass or just raise your hand.

   ▪ You will all have things that you wish to reveal and things that you prefer not to reveal to the group. You have the right to decide.

   ▪ Everyone in this group is feeling some anxiety. You are not the only one.

      ☞ *You may want to ask people to raise their hands if they are experiencing anxiety at that moment.*

   ▪ Participation in this group is an important first step in recovering from your anxiety. Just getting to this room and tolerating whatever anxiety you feel is a step in the right direction.

   ▪ Expect to feel some anxiety during this session. Think of it as an opportunity to begin to experience anxiety and to learn that you can function in the group even when you're anxious.

   ▪ As time goes on, more people will feel that they can speak during our group discussions; however, you all need to recognize that you can move forward at your own pace. The more you realize that your particular journey towards recovery is valid whether it is faster or slower than that of other group members, the more patience and understanding you will develop toward yourself during this process.

3. Distribute paper and pencils and introduce the sharing process with the following comments:

---

©1996 Whole Person Press 210 W Michigan Duluth MN 55802     (800) 247-6789

- Everyone has come to this group to work on recovering from their particular anxiety problems. Today, those who would like to do so will share their stories with the group.

- As you hear each other's stories, you will see that you have much in common. Anxiety, which is anxious apprehension or worry about some future event, and panic, which is concern about something one fears is just about to happen, are very frightening. Although your feelings of anxiety have similarities, each of you has a particular story to tell.

- As you learn about each other's anxiety story, notice similarities and differences in the stories. Record them on the paper that was distributed.

    ☞ *If you have experienced problems with anxiety, you may want to begin the process of sharing by revealing your own story. Depending on the composition of the group, this may or may not be appropriate.*

4. Ask for a volunteer to begin the process of sharing stories. Record the key points of each story on the easel paper. As people tell their stories, encourage them to state what they have tried up to now to rid themselves of their anxiety—what has worked, what has not worked. Throughout the storytelling, be prepared to write brief unifying comments regarding anxiety disorders on the easel paper.

5. After the stories are finished, lead a discussion about the similarities and differences that were noted.

6. Ask participants if they have any questions that they would like to ask you or each other about the stories they heard.

7. If time permits, ask people what they hope to receive from participation in the group.

8. Conclude by thanking participants for their courage in sharing their stories, reassuring those who did not speak that their presence in the group was valuable to them and to the group.

## Variations

- Form pairs and invite members of each pair to interview one another, then allow each interviewer to present details of the interviewee's anxiety problems.

- If the group is larger than six to ten participants, form smaller groups of two to three people. After allowing time for stories to be shared, ask each small group to describe its collective problems to the larger group.

- Have participants write their story, then ask volunteers to read as much as they wish of their own stories. This variation allows people to think through and write their entire story but to feel in control of how much they wish to reveal to the group.

# My Journal

Journals serve as an important treatment resource both in and out of group sessions. This exercise, which should take place during the first or second session, introduces the concept of journals.

## Goal

To establish a resource and start a practice that will continue to be useful after the group sessions are over.

## Group Size

Unlimited.

## Time

15 minutes.

## Materials

None.

## Participant Preparation

Pages 1–15 of *Overcoming Panic, Anxiety, & Phobias* will help participants prepare for this session and will reinforce what they learn during the session.

## Process

1. Introduce journaling as a helpful activity for people who are embarking on a journey.

   ■ Christina Baldwin wrote in *Life's Companion*: "Writing makes a map, and there is something about a journey that begs to have its passage marked."

   ■ Your journal can be a helpful companion and resource as you tackle your anxiety problem. Writing about your experiences will help you gain perspective on them and understand them.

It will also help you remember details and insights you might otherwise forget.

2. Lead a discussion of participants' experiences with journaling, using the following questions:

✔ Have you ever kept a journal or diary?

✔ What was it like to keep a journal?

✔ Did you encounter any difficulties in deciding what to write in your journal or in remembering to write in it?

✔ How do you think writing in a journal might be different at this point in your life?

3. Share with the group some practical hints about journaling.

■ Choose a book that feels inviting and unintimidating to you. You may be comfortable with a simple notebook like those you used in school. Or you may enjoy writing in a book with beautiful paper and cover.

■ You may find it convenient to keep parts of your journal on your computer. If so, you'll still need a notebook for the writing we'll do in group sessions and any other journaling you want to do away from your computer.

■ Some experiences and feelings may find expression more easily through drawing than through words. If you like to express yourself through drawing, keep your preferred art supplies—pastels, colored pencils, markers, charcoal—near your journal.

■ There is no right way to keep a journal. Perhaps you will prefer to set aside some time every day to reflect on the day's experiences, or perhaps you will find it more effective to jot down your thoughts and feelings soon after an important experience. Whatever it is that works best for you, make a contract with yourself to do it as consistently as you can.

4. Conclude by reminding participants that their journals will give them a written record of the progress they are making on their journey to recovery.

# What Is Anxiety?

During this exercise, people write down their questions about anxiety and begin to get answers. The session should be led by a mental health professional.

## Goals

To reduce stress—especially if this is an initial meeting.

To allow participants to become used to hearing their concerns voiced aloud.

To offer information regarding anxiety and panic.

To address concerns anonymously.

## Group Size

Unlimited.

## Time

1–2 hours.

## Materials

Pencils; 3 "x 5 " index cards; easel and easel paper; markers.

## Participant Preparation

Pages 1–15 of *Overcoming Panic, Anxiety, & Phobias* will help participants prepare for this session and will reinforce what they learn during the session.

## Process

1. Introduce the topic with the following comments:

   ▪ When excess anxiety or panic enters your life, it is understandable that you will have many questions and concerns. During this session, I will answer as many of your questions as time allows.

■ More questions will probably occur to you as you continue to work on your anxiety problems. Write them down, and we can discuss them during a future session.

2. Distribute several 3 "x 5 " index cards to each participant and give the following instructions:

➤ Write your questions about anxiety and panic on the cards, one question per card. Do not sign them.

➤ Give the cards back to me when you are done. I will read the questions anonymously.

3. Collect and shuffle the cards, then begin reading and answering the questions. You should be prepared for the questions listed in step 4, which are typically asked by people with anxiety problems. To feel fully prepared for any questions that participants may ask, it would be helpful for you to read *Overcoming Panic, Anxiety, & Phobias* as well as all the exercises in this manual. You'll want to be familiar enough with the material to be able to answer the questions in your own words. To help people focus, you may want to write the questions and the most significant phrases from your answers on the easel paper.

Either before or after you present your answer to a question, encourage participant involvement by asking questions such as:

✔ What information can you add from your own experience?

✔ What additional information would you like about this topic? And, if someone asks a question you don't know the answer to, acknowledge that to the group. Ask participants for ideas and/or promise to get the answer for the next session. Remember, you don't have to be perfect any more than your participants do.

4. The questions and answers listed below are typical of what participants might ask. You will want to be prepared for these questions and others.

**Question: What is an anxiety attack? What do you mean by that term?**

- An anxiety attack affects your body, your mind, and your behavior. During an attack, you become worried and anxious about something you believe will be dangerous in the future. Then your body and mind become focused on this fear.

- You may have physical sensations such as tension, shakiness, stomach distress, or sweating.

- You may find it difficult to stop worrying about this future danger that you are afraid will occur. If you are worried about certain themes such as your health or the well-being of loved ones, it may be hard to focus on anything else.

- Focusing on these concerns, you prepare yourself either by avoiding certain places and activities, by constantly checking to make sure you are safe, or by procrastinating because your excess worry is blocking concentration.

- The diagnostic manual that mental health professionals use categorizes worried thoughts and gives names to the condition associated with these thoughts. People with social phobias, for instance, fear being embarrassed in social situations. People with a generalized anxiety disorder often worry about issues such as health, physical danger, losing their job, and financial problems.

### Question: Why is this happening to me?

- We don't know exactly why some people have problems with anxiety while others do not, but researchers have begun to understand how anxiety disorders and their associated symptoms develop.

- Anxiety sufferers may have a genetic predisposition to anxiety. They may also tend to focus a great deal of attention on their internal state. When people who do not develop anxiety disorders have anxious thoughts, they can more easily refocus their attention away from their anxious thoughts and uncomfortable feelings and on to whatever's happening in their environment. It's interesting to note that many people will experience a panic attack during the year, become puzzled by

©1996 Whole Person Press 210 W Michigan Duluth MN 55802    (800) 247-6789

the unusual sensations but be able to shrug it off and go about their business. It's not that easy for someone who is prone to excess anxiety and panic. The extreme worry or uncomfortable sensations in their body are interpreted by them as signs that something is very wrong.

▪ People who develop anxiety disorders seem to be very good at noticing problems, but they have not developed strategies that they can count on to solve these problems.

▪ You may have grown up in a family where other people worried a lot and communicated their fears to you. On the other hand, they may have pushed you into stressful situations thinking that this process would toughen you.

▪ Anxiety and panic attacks can begin at times of illness, after people experience frightening reactions to drugs, after pregnancy, during or after relationship problems, when moving to a different home or changing jobs, after the death of a loved one, or during any period of great stress. Many people successfully endure periods of prolonged, intense stress, but the stress eventually takes its toll, and they develop excess anxiety after the stressful situation is over.

**Question: Are anxiety disorders increasing?**

▪ Although we don't know whether more people are suffering from anxiety disorders, we do know that more and more people are getting help with their anxiety problems. It is typical in the psychological field that as effective treatments are available, more people read about them in a newspaper or hear about them on the television and begin treatment.

**Question: How many people experience panic disorder?**

▪ During any given year, approximately one to two percent of the population will suffer from panic disorder.

**Question: What is the difference between anxiety and a phobia?**

▪ Anxiety ranges in intensity from mild to severe. Mild anxiety, which is normal and to be expected, helps prime the body for action.

■ However, when anxiety becomes intense and you become frightened of your thoughts or physical sensations, phobias may develop. There can be many causes for these phobias.

■ People with phobias understandably have learned to avoid situations they fear rather than to face them and the anxiety that they cause. Since avoidance reduces anxiety, they often begin avoiding more and more situations. For instance, people who feel embarrassed in certain social situations can develop a phobia to other settings in which they fear they may be humiliated.

■ This is particularly true of people who develop panic disorder accompanied by agoraphobia, the avoidance of all places where a panic attack might occur and escape or getting help seems difficult.

■ Although for many people, their phobia may be part of a larger anxiety disorder, some people who suffer from specific phobias do not experience excess anxiety unless they are in the situation that they fear. For example, people who are afraid that an airplane may crash, people who have a public speaking phobia, and people who are afraid of thunderstorms may only become anxious when forced to confront the situations they fear. They may not suffer from excess anxiety as long as they can avoid those specific situations.

■ Although some people learn to accept and live with their phobias, others find that their fears and the avoidance they trigger restricts their life unacceptably.

**Question: What are the symptoms associated with panic attacks?**

■ Panic attacks come on suddenly, occurring when the fight or flight response is set off in the body.

■ Typical symptoms of panic attacks include heart palpitations, flushing, sweating, shaking, choking sensations, stomach distress, dizziness, feelings of detachment or unreality, chills, and the fear of losing control, going crazy, or dying.

■ Typically, people fear most of all the panic episode itself. To protect themselves, they may avoid places where they believe it might occur.

**Question: What is panic disorder?**

■ People who suffer panic attacks are diagnosed as having a panic disorder when they have unexpected panic attacks, at least one of which is followed by at least one month of concern about experiencing more attacks, worry about what the attack means—for example, having a heart problem, losing control, and/or a change in behavior associated with the panic attack.

■ Prior to a panic attack, you may have had a lot of anxious apprehension. This anxiety primes your body for a fight or flight response that would be useful if there was really something to fear. The increased adrenaline, rapid heartbeat, muscle tension, and complete focus on dealing with danger that you experience could help you survive the attack.

■ Unfortunately, if there really isn't something to fear, the physical changes in your body make you a candidate for the onset of more panic attacks. The sensations themselves can be very scary. To protect yourself from these sensations, you may begin scanning your body, looking for the first signs that these uncomfortable feelings may occur. If you notice any symptoms, your fear helps cause them to increase, and that causes more fear. You may then develop an ongoing panic disorder.

**Question: How can you control these reactions? They just seem to keep happening. It's very discouraging.**

■ Anxiety and panic attacks are extremely discouraging. It's important to keep in mind that your physical sensations, if you are experiencing panic, are very real. They are not just in your mind.

■ We can confidently state that researchers around the country have developed a variety of strategies that can significantly reduce anxiety and panic symptoms and, in many cases, eliminate them.

■ Anxiety in itself is not a problem. Anxiety serves a natural function. We all experience anxiety; it helps prime us in situations where we need to be a little more excited. And panic is a survival mechanism when there's really something to fear.

■ People who experience excessive anxiety and panic need to systematically learn coping strategies that will enable them to challenge their thoughts, to relax their bodies, and to begin exposing themselves to situations that they have been avoiding.

**Question: What is cognitive therapy and how can it help me?**

■ Cognitive therapy helps people to become aware of the relationship between their thoughts, their behavior, and their environment. It is useful for the treatment of anxiety disorders because it helps people examine their thoughts and look for the evidence for and against their fearful predictions. If you have been predicting that a disaster will occur, for instance, you will be asked to rationally examine the likelihood that it will happen, the potential consequences if it does occur, and your ability to cope with these consequences.

■ Your anxiety will lessen when you recognize that the event is not very likely to happen and that you would be able to cope if it did occur.

**Question: Can physical illnesses cause anxiety?**

■ People who suffer from anxiety should see a physician, discuss all their symptoms, and get a thorough physical examination. The physician will determine whether the symptoms are caused by a physical condition, are an emotional response to a physical condition, or are unrelated to any physical condition.

■ A number of physical conditions such as thyroid or cardiac problems can cause symptoms that might be attributed to anxiety.

■ Other medical conditions such as asthma have frightening

symptoms. The breathing problems associated with an asthma attack can trigger a panic attack.

■ The fear of suffering a second heart attack can cause extreme anxiety even if there is little risk of an attack occurring. The physical and emotional effects of cancer and chemotherapy can also cause anxiety or panic.

■ Heavy coffee drinkers and substance abusers can experience panic symptoms.

**Question: Are anxiety attacks the outward symptoms of more serious psychological disorders? Can my symptoms cause me to lose control of myself?**

■ Many anxiety sufferers become particularly frightened by their feelings of loss of control. They may recognize that their fears are irrational and become more and more concerned that they will completely lose control of themselves and end up in an mental institution. Anxiety problems, however, do not lead to a total loss of control.

■ As people participate in an anxiety treatment program, they will discover that although their sensations are frightening and uncomfortable, their natural responses will protect them, and they will not lose complete control.

**Question: How can family and friends help?**

■ It's important to be supportive, to try to learn as much as you can about your loved one's specific anxiety disorder, and to listen to how they feel you could be of help to them.

■ Some people just want to talk about the problem and have someone be sympathetic. Others want their loved ones to take a more active part in the treatment. The best rule of thumb is to ask the person with the anxiety.

## Variation

■ Collect the cards on which questions were written in step 2. Shuffle and redistribute them, then allow participants to read one another's questions as you answer them.

# Breaking Free from the Worry and Panic Cycles

Participants analyze the cycles of worry and panic and strategize about how they can intervene. The session should be led by a mental health professional.

## Goals

To educate participants about the cycles of worry and panic.

To help people break self-defeating patterns by analyzing them.

To build hope that recovery is possible.

## Group Size

Unlimited.

## Time

1–3 hours. If time is limited, review the worry cycle in one session and the panic cycle in a second session. Conclude each session with the affirmation in step 3 on page 23.

## Materials

Pencils; paper; easel and easel paper; markers; **The Worry Cycle** worksheet; **The Panic Cycle** worksheet.

## Participant Preparation

Pages 11–14 of *Overcoming Panic, Anxiety, & Phobias* will help participants prepare for this session and will reinforce what they learn during the session.

> ☞ *The information presented in this session is very important and should be reinforced throughout therapy. Anxiety sufferers need to become aware of the specific situations in which they are anxious and the thoughts, physical sensations, and behaviors that accompany their anxiety episodes.*

---

*Because each of these components will be addressed during therapy, they need to be able to describe their anxiety episodes in terms of these components.*

## Process

## The Worry Cycle

1. Introduce the worry cycle by copying the diagram below on easel paper.

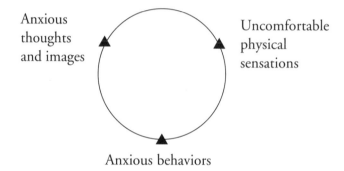

Anxious thoughts and images

Uncomfortable physical sensations

Anxious behaviors

2. One at a time, touch each of the entry points to the worry cycle and follow the circle as you describe how the following three people, all of them anxious about their job performance, entered the worry cycle.

- Bonnie began by imagining in vivid detail a disastrous performance evaluation. Tension headaches followed, and she became curt and rude to customers . . . which caused her to worry even more about her evaluation.

- Mike, also facing an annual performance interview, began feeling sick to his stomach each morning. He began taking a variety of stomach medications, but he worried that if his supervisor noticed, he would look even more inadequate than he felt . . . and he felt even more sick.

- Jon began obsessively reviewing all his work to make sure that it was absolutely perfect. He still worried that he had not done enough, and he found that his vision often seemed blurred, which made it hard to concentrate . . . so he felt that he had to go over his work again.

3. Help participants begin to differentiate between realistic and excessive worry by making the following points:

   ■ Everyone worries.

   ■ Worry protects us by encouraging us to be cautious and process risk.

   ■ However, when we begin to worry about some future disaster occurring and can't turn off our anxiety, worry can begin to take over our lives.

   ■ The worry cycle may start with some type of anxious thought about a future threat.

   ■ We may notice that we're becoming tense or having some other physical sensation of anxiety, then begin to have worry thoughts.

   ■ Before we even notice our unrealistic worry and uncomfortable sensations, we may find ourselves behaving in an anxious manner.

   ■ This circle of worried thoughts, unpleasant physical sensations, and anxious behaviors goes round and round. You can enter it at any point.

4. Encourage participants to begin understanding their own worry cycle by asking the questions listed below. Record participants' responses on easel paper under the headings "thoughts," "physical sensations," and "behaviors."

   ✔ What thoughts go through your mind when you begin worrying about something that may happen in the future?

   ✔ What uncomfortable physical sensations do you have?

   ✔ What are your anxious behaviors?

5. Distribute The Worry Cycle worksheet and give participants 10 minutes to complete it.

©1996 Whole Person Press 210 W Michigan Duluth MN 55802    (800) 247-6789

☞ *Some people may have trouble describing their anxiety episodes by using this method. If this is the case, ask them to think of an incident in which they were anxious and to run it by in their mind as if they were watching a movie. Reassure them that with increased awareness the process becomes easier.*

6. Ask participants who are willing to share the responses on their worksheets with the group. Add any new ideas to the list you have been developing on the easel paper.

## The Panic Cycle

1. Introduce the panic cycle by making the following comments:
   - Many people, in addition to worrying excessively about events in the future, also experience panic attacks.
   - Symptoms of panic attacks can occur with any anxiety disorder and may actually be a part of that anxiety disorder.
   - Many of you find yourself only in the worry cycle, but others may be in the worry cycle and also in the panic cycle.

2. Prepare to explain the panic cycle by copying the diagram below on easel paper.

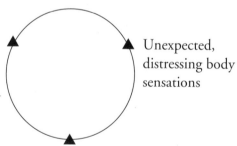

Fearful thoughts or images of immediate danger

Unexpected, distressing body sensations

The urge to avoid the situation, to distract oneself, or to flee

3. Ask participants to recall a time when they were in real danger and to ask themselves the following questions:
   ✔ What were my thoughts or images?

---

✔ How did I feel? What distressing body sensations did I have?

✔ What actions did I take or want to take?

4. Ask one or more of the participants to volunteer to share their experience with the group.

   ☞ *If people relate events that were not actually dangerous but were false alarms, encourage them to think about the triggering event, their thoughts, physical sensations, actions, and the actual evidence of danger. These episodes can be discussed later in the session.*

5. If necessary, supplement the participants' stories with an illustration such as the one that follows:

   ▪ Imagine that torrential rains are pouring down and your house begins to become flooded. You notice that the water level is rising. There are disaster warnings on the radio and television.

   ▪ Your body sets off the flight or fight response. The flight or fight response is a wonderful mechanism that is designed to protect us from harm. During this response, various hormones are secreted in your body. You become focused on getting to a safe spot, and your heart may start to beat more rapidly to propel you to escape. You may start shaking, but you will concentrate on leaving the area and keeping your loved ones safe.

6. Contrast this response to a real disaster with a panic attack by making the following comments:

   ▪ During panic attacks you'll experience the same kinds of frightening physical sensations. As you say to your self, "I've got to get out of here right now!" your body becomes more and more distressed. You might start shaking or sweating and experience heart palpitations or other panic sensations. You will focus on getting yourself out as quickly and safely as possible.

   ▪ When you are in the midst of a panic attack, your thoughts, physical sensations, and actions are the same as when you are in real danger. However, in these cases, where no real danger is involved, we call the reaction a false alarm.

■ When this false alarm is set off more than once you become more and more concerned, more and more frightened that it will happen again.

■ Although the danger may not be real, the uncomfortable sensations you feel are absolutely real. As a step toward recovery, you need to begin analyzing your feelings, thoughts, and actions, as well as the likelihood of real danger.

7. Encourage participants to begin understanding their own panic cycle by asking the questions listed below. Record participants' responses on easel paper under the headings "thoughts," "physical sensations," and "behaviors."

✔ What fearful thoughts and images are in your mind at the onset of or during a panic attack?

✔ What unexpected, distressing, even terrifying physical sensations do you have?

✔ In what ways do your behaviors demonstrate the urge to flee from your thoughts and uncomfortable body sensations as well as from the situation? Are there other ways in which your behaviors are a reaction to your fears—for example, do you pace or keep checking to make sure everything is OK?

8. Distribute **The Panic Cycle** worksheet and give participants 10 minutes to complete it.

9. Ask participants who are willing to share the responses on their worksheets with the group. Add any new ideas to the list you have been developing on the easel paper.

10. Because just talking about these situations can be anxiety provoking, the group will be more comfortable if you acknowledge this fact by asking participants to respond to the following questions with a show of hands:

✔ How many of you have found that your anxiety level has risen during this discussion?

✔ Have you had some uncomfortable physical sensations?

11. Demonstrate understanding and acceptance of participants' feelings by making the following points:

   ■ For people who suffer from excess anxiety or panic attacks, just thinking about these scenarios is enough to cause the beginnings of an attack.

   ■ People with anxiety problems have conditioned their bodies to respond quickly to thoughts of danger just as though the danger is actually happening.

   ■ Your feelings are very natural. Your mind and body have become extremely sensitized and produce excess anxiety or panic when facing scary thoughts or sensations.

   ■ Since you need to gain evidence that anxiety sensations are uncomfortable, but not really dangerous, I encourage those of you who are feeling an increase in anxiety to see this as an opportunity to gain evidence that your thoughts are extremely powerful, but that they don't always predict danger.

## Breaking free from the worry and panic cycles

1. Introduce the need to break free of the worry cycle and the panic cycle by making the following points:

   ■ As you can see from the drawings and from comments of group members, the worry cycle and the panic cycle are closed circles.

   ■ We become prisoners within these circles to uncontrollable worry and, in some cases, to panic.

   ■ Activities that we once carried out in comfort, we may find terrifying, and more and more activities and situations become closed to us. Worry replaces pleasure.

   ■ We experience even our own bodies as dangerous when the

physical sensations associated with exercise, emotion, or sex become frightening in themselves.

■ As hard as we try to break out of the circles, nothing seems to work. Or a technique may sometimes work and sometimes not work, which is confusing and discouraging.

■ We may have learned to reduce our distress by avoiding a great many things in a desperate attempt to contain our anxiety. This may lower our anxiety and panic temporarily, but we are still trapped in the cycle.

2. Encourage participants to take notes as you outline the key recovery steps on the easel paper.

■ The first step toward recovery is for you to gain an understanding of what is happening to you. You are already doing this by participating in this group and by reading about your problem.

■ The next step will be to continue to analyze your specific triggers to anxiety or panic. You will rate your level of anxiety from zero, the calmest you have ever been, to ten, the most anxious or panicky you have ever felt. You will note your specific thoughts, physical sensations, and actions.

As you break your stress into these components, you will be able to develop and use the coping strategies that are part of a complete program of recovery. Once you have identified what your physical sensations, thoughts, and actions are, you can begin to analyze what you are basing your fear reactions on. You can then begin to do some experiments to test your conclusions. As you continue you will gain coping skills that will enable you to begin to gradually challenge your anxious thoughts and relax your body. You can feel less tension and begin to let go of any behaviors such as avoidance, checking to see if everything is OK, or distraction that are maintaining your fears. You will learn these coping strategies within this group.

3. Conclude the session by making the following comments:

- Look at your copies of **The Worry Cycle** and **The Panic Cycle** worksheets. Circle any point on the worry cycle where you feel you might have a chance of breaking through. If you also experience panic attacks, complete the same process on **The Panic Cycle** worksheet. Keep these worksheets; as you learn more in group meetings, you will develop coping strategies that will help you make these breakthroughs.

- During the coming week, become aware of when you are feeling anxiety or panic. At that very moment, take note of the situation, your anxious thoughts or images, physical sensations, and behaviors, and record them on your worksheets. This process is a first step to gaining control over what appear to be uncontrollable symptoms.

- Congratulate yourself on coming to this meeting. It's not easy to come to a group meeting and to talk about things that stir up your anxiety. Just doing that is an important step in breaking out of these anxiety cycles. I wish you luck on your journey and recovery.

## Variation

- If you have only 20 minutes, distribute **The Worry Cycle** and **The Panic Cycle** worksheets. Tell participants to think about how they experience each stage of the worry and panic cycles, to write a few notes to describe each stage as they experience it, and to draw an arrow or circle to the place in the cycle where they think they can start to break free.

## THE WORRY CYCLE

Fill in your specific worry cycle below:

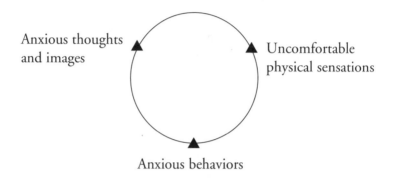

Anxious thoughts
and images

Uncomfortable
physical sensations

Anxious behaviors

### My Worry Cycle

My thoughts or images are _____

_____

_____

_____

_____

My physical sensations are _____

_____

_____

_____

My actions are _____

_____

_____

_____

# THE PANIC CYCLE

Fill in your specific panic cycle below:

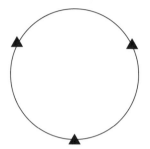

Fearful thoughts
or images of
immediate
danger

Intense and
distressing body
sensations

The urge to avoid the
situation, to distract
oneself, and to flee

## My Panic Cycle

My panic attacks are triggered by _____

_____

My physical sensations are _____

_____

_____

My thoughts and images are _____

_____

_____

My actions are _____

_____

Other activities and places that I now fear include _____

_____

_____

_____

©1996 Whole Person Press 210 W Michigan Duluth MN 55802      (800) 247-6789

# Anxiety and Panic Attacks— Yours, Mine, Ours

Although the situations that arouse anxiety and panic attacks may be different for each person, anxiety problems have common characteristics. During this exercise, participants discuss these characteristics and identify the physical symptoms, thoughts, and behaviors that accompany them.

## Goals

To create a sense of identification and mutual support among participants.

To become aware of likenesses and differences among members' anxiety and panic problems.

To introduce distinctions between various types of anxiety prior to introducing coping strategies for each.

## Group Size

Unlimited.

## Time

30–60 minutes.

## Materials

Pencils; paper; easel and easel paper; markers.

## Participant Preparation

Pages 1–10 of *Overcoming Panic, Anxiety, & Phobias* will help participants prepare for this session and will reinforce what they learn during the session.

## Process

1. Introduce the exercise by telling participants that although they

may feel quite alone with their anxiety problem, many other people struggle with similar problems.

2. Invite the group to suggest different characteristics of their anxiety and panic problems. As the characteristics are mentioned, list them on the easel paper under three headings: physical sensations that occur when I am anxious, thoughts that precede or are brought about by anxiety, and behaviors that occur as a result of anticipated or actual anxiety.

3. When the list seems complete, summarize by stating that when anxiety becomes excessive or panic attacks occur, they can take over people's lives, rob them of satisfaction, and imprison them.

4. Ask the group to spend 10 minutes listing ways in which anxiety is keeping them from living life fully and freely.

5. Ask participants who are willing to share their responses with the group.

6. Encourage participants to visualize how they could free themselves of the debilitating effects of severe anxiety. Ask them to close their eyes while you slowly read the script that follows:

> *Imagine that you are caught in a trap, held fast in a strong net that leaves you little freedom to move and, apparently, no way to escape. Notice your fear and frustration as you struggle unsuccessfully to free yourself. Now, begin to calm yourself as you slowly breathe in . . . and out . . . in . . . and out. Imagine yourself becoming calm and relaxed. As you continue to breathe slowly and smoothly, begin to focus on the net that binds you, looking for weak threads that you could break. If you begin feeling tense, focus again on your slow, smooth breathing. When you feel relaxed but ready, begin breaking the weakest threads, one at a time, until you can step free from the net. You may be feeling so discouraged that you can't imagine yourself breaking through. If so, don't struggle to create that image. Instead, continue to relax,*

*breathing slowly and evenly, knowing that someday you will feel ready to begin breaking the threads that bind you.*

7. Form groups of two to four participants and ask members of these small groups to spend 5 minutes sharing with each other the benefits of freeing themselves from excess anxiety or panic attacks and the ways in which this will change their lives.

8. Reconvene the entire group and ask each participant to make a positive statement about the benefit of recovery by completing the following statement: When I am free of excess anxiety or panic attacks, I will be able to . . .

9. Conclude the session by commending participants for their willingness to share their struggles with other members of the group.

©1996 Whole Person Press 210 W Michigan Duluth MN 55802      (800) 247-6789

# How I Experience Anxiety

This self-assessment uses standard diagnostic criteria to help participants determine what kind of anxiety is affecting them. The session should be led by a mental health professional.

## Goal

To help people identify the specific type of anxiety affecting them.

## Group Size

Unlimited.

## Time

1 hour.

## Materials

Pencils; paper; easel and easel paper; markers.

## Participant Preparation

Pages 1–3, 15–18 of *Overcoming Panic, Anxiety, & Phobias* will help participants prepare for this session and will reinforce what they learn during the session.

## Process

1. Introduce the exercise by explaining that understanding the ways in which we are affected by anxiety can help us overcome it.

2. Distribute blank paper and ask participants to number the paper from 1 to 45. Provide the following instructions:

   ➤ The characteristics associated with anxiety vary from person to person. I am going to read a list of some of these characteristics. They are divided into six categories. If a characteristic applies to you, place a Y (for yes) to the right of the number on your paper. If a characteristic does not apply to you, enter an N (for no).

©1996 Whole Person Press 210 W Michigan Duluth MN 55802     (800) 247-6789

➤ Think about how anxiety has affected you during the past year. Have you experienced any of the following symptoms?

1) Palpitations, pounding heart, fast heart rate

2) Sweating

3) Trembling or shaking

4) Sensations of shortness of breath or smothering

5) Feelings of choking

6) Chest pain or discomfort

7) Nausea or stomach distress

8) Feelings of dizziness, unsteadiness, light-headedness, or faintness

9) Feelings of unreality or of being detached from yourself

10) Fear of losing control or going crazy

11) Fear of dying

12) Numbness or tingling sensations

13) Chills or hot flashes

If you have had at least four of the previously listed feelings in a short period of time, you may have been having a panic attack.

14) Have you had one or more panic attacks out of the blue?

15) Have you worried repeatedly for a month or more about having another panic attack?

16) When you panic, is your greatest fear that you might go crazy, have a heart attack, or lose control?

17) Do you monitor yourself to detect tiny changes in your physical sensations, trying to prevent being caught unaware by a panic attack?

18) Do you scan places you enter to see where the exits are, in case you might have a panic attack and have the urge to escape?

19) Have these frightening episodes changed your life?

If some of the prior questions describe you, you may have a panic disorder.

20) In addition to having had panic sensations, do you avoid or suffer through situations where you fear having a panic attack, particularly if escape may seem difficult or embarrassing?

21) Is it easier for you to enter these situations with a trusted companion?

22) Here are some examples of situations that are difficult to leave easily: getting your hair cut, driving, visiting the dentist, standing in lines, eating in restaurants, going to shopping malls, theaters, or church. Are you especially frightened of being in any of these or similar situations?

If you answered yes to some of the preceding questions, you may have developed agoraphobia.

23) Do you suffer from a dread of something quite specific that most others are not as worried about? It doesn't matter what that specific thing or situation is; examples include flying, heights, enclosed spaces, an animal, needles, or seeing blood.

24) Are you unaffected by excess anxiety in other areas of your life, but feel a sense of terror when approaching the thing or situation you fear?

25) Do you try to avoid such things or situations?

26) Does your anticipation, avoidance, and distress in these situations interfere with your life in significant ways?

If the previous descriptions apply to you, you may be experiencing a specific phobia.

27) Are you bewildered by the strange and exaggerated physical responses you experience in social situations?

28) Do you dread returning to these situations?

29) Do you worry about behaving in a way you find humiliating or that might cause others to think less of you?

30) Do you feel you are not making the kind of impression on others that you long to make?

31) Are you convinced that people think less of you because they see signs of nervousness?

32) Do these worries constrict your ability to live the way you want, with freedom and confidence?

33) Do you avoid eating or socializing for fear that others will notice that your hands are shaking or that you're blushing or sweating?

34) Do you dread situations where you feel evaluated or scrutinized by others, such as public speaking, performance situations, being the center of attention, being watched while you work?

Saying yes to several of the prior questions may indicate that your problem is a social phobia.

35) Have you answered no to most of the previous questions but still feel that anxiety is a big factor in your life?

36) Does your mind tend to focus on the negative?

37) Do you feel restless, keyed-up, and find it hard to relax?

38) Do you notice that if one worry leaves you, another one tends to take its place?

39) Do you pay attention to things that feed your worries and discount things that reassure other people?

40) Do people tell you to relax?

41) Do you wish you could be free of these worries, and try to, but find it difficult or impossible?

42) Do you notice that a lot of what you worry about doesn't happen or if it does, it's not as bad as you thought?

©1996 Whole Person Press 210 W Michigan Duluth MN 55802      (800) 247-6789

43) Do you sometimes have a feeling that bad events don't occur because you've been worrying about them?

44) Are you tired, tense, overloaded, or always afraid you won't get everything done?

45) Do you have trouble sleeping—either falling asleep, staying asleep, or sleeping soundly?

Saying yes to several of the preceding questions suggests that you may have a generalized anxiety disorder.

3. Ask participants to share their reactions to finding a name for their particular anxiety disorder. Encourage them to understand that identifying their problem is the first step toward solving it.

©1996 Whole Person Press 210 W Michigan Duluth MN 55802     (800) 247-6789

# My Goals

This exercise is essential for people with anxiety problems. Those with intense social phobias are introduced to the group process in a nonthreatening way by writing their thoughts, hopes, and aspirations before they have to speak about them. The therapist should be prepared to define what a goal is and what an achievable goal is, and to suggest that specific steps to achieve what might otherwise seem an impossible dream will be supplied later. The session should be led by a mental health professional.

**Goals**

To reinforce each participant's sense that success might actually be possible.

To reduce the stress of an initial meeting.

To allow participants to become used to hearing their concerns voiced aloud.

**Group Size**

Unlimited.

**Time**

1–2 hours.

**Materials**

Pencils; 3 "x 5 "index cards; **My Goals** worksheet.

**Participant Preparation**

Pages 19, 20 of *Overcoming Panic, Anxiety, & Phobias* will help participants prepare for this session and will reinforce what they learn during the session.

**Process**

1. Introduce the exercise by asking the following questions, which

©1996 Whole Person Press 210 W Michigan Duluth MN 55802      (800) 247-6789

will help participants distinguish between wishes and goals and between realistic and unrealistic goals. As they list their wishes and goals, write them on the easel paper in two columns, one for wishes and one for goals.

✔ When you were a child, you probably had lots of wishes and dreams. What were some of these wishes?

✔ What wishes and dreams do you have as an adult?

✔ Goals are different from wishes. What are your goals in life?

✔ What specific goals do you have in relation to recovery from your anxiety disorder?

2. Review the list of goals that you have written on the easel paper, asking participants to decide whether each goal is realistic or unrealistic. Put a "0" next to those that are unrealistic, a "+" next to those that seem to be realistic.

3. Present the following information about goal-setting, pausing after each point to encourage discussion:

   ■ Anxiety and panic attacks can seem so overwhelming that it becomes very difficult to focus on specific goals.

   ■ It's understandable that what each of you wants to do is just get rid of your anxiety—right now!

   ■ However, as anxiety attacks continue, goal-setting becomes an important procedure that helps break up what seems to be an overwhelming task into several manageable steps.

   ■ As you think of some goals that you would like to reach within the next month, try to make them realistic. For example, the goal of ridding oneself of all anxiety would be unrealistic. Everyone experiences some anxiety.

   ■ It may be helpful to ask yourself how you will know that you are making progress in this group. Many times the answer to that question will help you set your goals.

4. By asking the following questions, encourage participants to recognize that a long-standing and serious problem cannot be solved overnight:

©1996 Whole Person Press 210 W Michigan Duluth MN 55802     (800) 247-6789

✔ Many of you have suffered from anxiety or panic for a long time. How long have you had these symptoms?

✔ Even those who have recently developed anxiety attacks may be experiencing some major impacts from their anxiety problems. Is this happening to you?

5. Continue by making the following comments about the desire for rapid recovery:

   ▪ Of course you all want to recover as quickly as possible.

   ▪ I encourage you, however, to set up a plan for long term recovery—one that you will be able to rely on in the future during times of stress, one that you can systematically learn and which, through practice, will become an automatic response.

6. Distribute the **My Goals** worksheet and ask participants to spend 10 minutes completing the list of goals in light of the previous discussion of realistic goals. (Action steps will be filled out as coping strategies are learned.)

7. Ask for volunteers to read their goals, writing them on easel paper as they are read. When they have all been listed, spend 10 minutes discussing them, making sure each goal is specific and realistic and modifying them if necessary. If participants are still having difficulty with this process, offer a few examples such as:

   ▪ I will feel 50 percent less fear when driving up hills.

   ▪ I will continue to stay in the supermarket even when I am experiencing some anxiety.

   ▪ I will look at a picture of a cat until my anxiety level lowers.

8. Encourage participants to view these initial goals as a beginning by making the following comments:

   ▪ Recovering from anxiety will go more smoothly if you set realistic goals and then, when you have reached those goals, review your progress and set additional goals.

- Setting realistic goals will help you recognize the progress you are making on your journey to recovery.

## Variation

- After participants complete the **My Goals** worksheet, have them form pairs and interview one another. Then reconvene the groups and ask them to present each other's goals.

# MY GOALS

List two to four goals you'd like to achieve in the next one to three months. Fill in the action strategies as you learn coping skills.

Goal 1 _____

Action strategies to achieve my goal:

    a. _____

    b. _____

    c. _____

    d. _____

Goal 2 _____

Action strategies to achieve my goal:

    a. _____

    b. _____

    c. _____

    d. _____

Goal 3 _____

Action strategies to achieve my goal:

    a. _____

    b. _____

    c. _____

    d. _____

Goal 4 _____

Action strategies to achieve my goal:

    a. _____

    b. _____

    c. _____

    d. _____

# Rating My Anxiety

This mini-lecture and demonstration introduces participants to the benefits of rating their anxiety. This session should be used prior to teaching relaxation techniques.

## Goals

To introduce the concept that anxiety is experienced at different levels at different times.

To give members a tool for assessing their level of anxiety.

## Group Size

Unlimited.

## Time

20 minutes.

## Materials

Easel and easel paper; markers; pencils; paper; **Anxiety Rating Scale** worksheets.

## Participant Preparation

Pages 17, 18 of *Overcoming Panic, Anxiety, & Phobias* will help participants prepare for this session and will reinforce what they learn during the session.

## Process

1. Introduce the session by acknowledging that participants may feel somewhat anxious about discussing their problems in a group. Give the following instructions:

   ➤ If you are feeling even a little bit anxious or uncomfortable, please raise your hand.

   ➤ Analyze your feelings and body sensations, rating them on a scale from 0 to 10, with 0 being total calm and 10 being the worst feeling of panic you have ever experienced.

➤ I'm going to call out numbers from 0 to 10. Raise your hand when I call out the number that best seems to identify your feelings right now. I'll record the ratings on the easel. Let's begin. Raise your hand if you rated your anxiety at 0—total calm . . .

2. Continue by describing the value of being able to identify varying levels of anxiety.

- When people become extremely worried about their feelings of anxiety and fearful about possible panic attacks, they often fail to differentiate between mild and severe anxiety. As soon as they recognize any uncomfortable feelings, they focus on these feelings so intensely that their anxiety immediately escalates.

- Rating your anxiety level will help you learn that sometimes anxiety is milder and more easily controlled.

- Recognizing mild anxiety will enable you to intervene with techniques such as calm breathing. These relaxation techniques can successfully prevent mild anxiety from escalating into a severe attack.

- Just as we did in our group a few moments ago, you can assign a number to any anxiety that you feel. Once you are aware that your levels of anxiety vary in intensity, you will be able to use this anxiety rating technique to assess how you feel. Instead of reacting to mild anxiety unconsciously in ways that cause it to get worse, you can take time to consciously respond in ways that calm you.

- Let's imagine that you become anxious in social situations and you have to attend a gathering where you experience mild heart palpitations or slight shakiness—level 3, for example. If you are not paying attention, you may begin to take short, shallow breaths that exaggerate your symptoms. If, instead, you recognize that you are having a mild reaction and remember that a less anxious response is possible, you can begin using some of the relaxation methods you're learning. Techniques such as slowing your breathing can dramatically reduce the physical symptoms of anxiety and help avert a spiral of worsening anxiety.

3. Distribute the **Anxiety Rating Scale** worksheets and give the following instructions:

   ➤ On the worksheets that I am distributing, please record, as specifically as possible, the thoughts, body sensations, and behaviors that accompany varying levels of anxiety.

   ➤ You will have about 10 minutes to complete the worksheets. The information on it will be used in other sessions; the worksheets will be yours to keep.

4. When participants appear to be done writing, ask those who are willing to share some of their responses. Record them on the easel paper in columns numbered 10, 8, 6, 4, and 2.

5. Lead a discussion of the varying levels of anxiety shown by responses on the easel paper. Encourage participants to recognize the following points:

   ■ Thoughts, body sensations, and behaviors vary dramatically at different levels of anxiety.

   ■ Interventions that will work at low anxiety levels may not be effective at higher levels. For instance, it is easier to listen to your rational self when you are still feeling relatively calm. Therefore, early intervention is important.

   ■ Even extreme anxiety eventually drops. Your worst fears do not come true.

6. Conclude the session by encouraging participants to rate their anxiety level at different times every day prior to the next session.

# ANXIETY RATING SCALE

Many people can't discriminate between different levels of anxiety or panic. They feel either calm or anxious. To help you become aware of your own intermediate levels of anxiety, complete this worksheet, being as specific as you can.

As you experiment with the coping strategies you will be learning, refer to this worksheet in order to discover what strategies work best for you at different levels of anxiety.

### Level 10: extreme anxiety

When my anxiety is at level 10, my thoughts are _____

_____

_____

My body sensations are _____

_____

_____

My behaviors include _____

_____

### Level 8: on the verge of extreme anxiety

When my anxiety is at level 8, my thoughts are _____

_____

_____

My body sensations are _____

_____

_____

My behaviors include _____

_____

©1996 Whole Person Press 210 W Michigan Duluth MN 55802　　　(800) 247-6789

## Level 6: severe anxiety

When my anxiety is at level 6, my thoughts are _____

_____

_____

My body sensations are _____

_____

_____

My behaviors include _____

_____

## Level 4: moderate anxiety

When my anxiety is at level 4, my thoughts are _____

_____

_____

My body sensations are _____

_____

_____

My behaviors include _____

_____

## Level 2: mild anxiety

When my anxiety is at level 2, my thoughts are _____

_____

_____

My body sensations are _____

_____

_____

My behaviors include _____

_____

# What Is Happening to Me?

This exercise encourages participants to view their anxiety episodes dispassionately by helping them examine the anatomy of a typical anxiety episode. Although looking closely at an anxiety episode may seem scary, confidence increases rapidly, making this process well worth the effort. The session should be led by a mental health professional.

## Goals

To encourage participants to view their anxiety more objectively.

To allow participants to become used to observing their anxiety episodes directly.

To reinforce each participant's confidence.

## Group Size

Unlimited.

## Time

1 hour.

## Materials

Pencils; easel and easel paper; **Anxiety and Panic Responses** worksheet.

## Participant Preparation

Pages 3–8 of *Overcoming Panic, Anxiety, & Phobias* will help participants prepare for this session and will reinforce what they learn during the session.

## Process

1. Introduce the session by asking participants to help you tell a story about one person's anxiety. Use their responses to write the

story on easel paper. Begin the story by saying that Peggy is waiting for her daughter, Jan, to return from a date. Jan's curfew is midnight. It is now 12:15 A.M. Peggy worries a lot about Jan, so she's beginning to feel very anxious.

✔ What are Peggy's worst worries and predictions of doom?

✔ What uncomfortable, perhaps frightening, physical sensations does she have?

✔ What does Peggy do as a result of her fears?

2. Ask participants who are willing to share their own stories of a particular episode of anxiety or panic. Ask them to be specific about the situation or other anxiety triggers, their thoughts, their physical sensations, and their behaviors. Record the information on easel paper in four columns using the four headings listed above.

3. Encourage participants to take note of the variety of anxiety triggers, thoughts, sensations, and behaviors. Help them also to recognize similarities by talking about the following points:

▪ What is bothersome or frightening to one person may not be to another.

▪ However, if you believe that something dangerous is going to happen immediately or in the future, your body will respond with a variety of uncomfortable physical sensations.

▪ These sensations help bring about more anxiety or panic.

▪ Anxiety occurs when you become tense, preoccupied, and apprehensive about some future threat. Performance is affected as your ability to focus on current tasks diminishes. Panic arises when you become fearful about an immediate threat, experience strong physiological sensations, and wish to escape from the situation.

▪ Depending on your specific anxiety problem, you may try to control this process by worrying more, by escaping from the situation, or by trying to keep the situation from ever happening again.

4. Advise participants that analyzing their thoughts, physical sensations, and actions during an anxiety or panic attack is a first step towards managing them. The most effective way to conduct this analysis is to record the symptoms in writing.

5. Distribute the **Anxiety and Panic Responses** worksheet. Give the following instructions:

   ➤ Describe a typical anxiety or panic episode that you have experienced. What brought on your anxiety attack or triggered your panic? Rate your anxiety level from 0 to 10.

   ➤ After describing the episode itself, note the associated thoughts, physical sensations, and behaviors, each under a separate heading on the worksheet.

   ☞ *If participants have difficulty with this process, ask them to close their eyes and imagine the episode, running it through their minds like a movie. Let them know that this process will become easier with practice and increased awareness of all the variables involved in maintaining their anxiety problem.*

6. Conclude by encouraging participants to analyze several other episodes of anxiety or panic prior to the next session.

## Variations

■ Allow participants to work in teams of two or three people, asking each other detailed questions in order to solicit more information and in order to reinforce the sense that they are not alone.

■ Use examples that illustrate a range of anxiety disorders—social phobias, specific phobias, agoraphobia, panic disorder, etc. Excerpts from the recovery stories in *Overcoming Panic, Anxiety, & Phobias* could provide these examples.

# ANXIETY AND PANIC RESPONSES

## Part I: Anxiety producing episode

Date _____          Time _____

What brought on your feelings of anxiety or panic?

_____

_____

Circle your anxiety level:

0     1     2     3     4     5     6     7     8     9     10

   none            mild          moderate      strong

## Part II: Anxiety and panic responses

a. Physical sensations

List the physical sensations you felt during your anxiety response, e.g., dizziness, shortness of breath, blushing, sweating, muscle tension. Circle the three that frighten you most.

_____

_____

b. Thoughts and images

List the thoughts you had when anticipating or experiencing your anxiety response, e.g., "I'm having a heart attack," "I'm losing control," or "Something terrible will happen."

_____

_____

c. Behaviors and actions

List the behaviors you exhibited or actions you took as a result of your anxiety response. _____

_____

©1996 Whole Person Press 210 W Michigan Duluth MN 55802     (800) 247-6789

# Progressive Muscle Relaxation

Participants learn to recognize feelings of tension and relaxation in their bodies by practicing a progressive muscle relaxation exercise. They note the effect that relaxation has on their anxiety level.

## Goals

To experience the state of deep relaxation.

To prepare participants to practice relaxation on their own.

To offer participants an experience of relaxation to compare with their usual body tension.

## Group Size

Unlimited.

## Time

30 minutes.

## Materials

Tape recorder and tape of soothing music; pencils; **Tension/Relaxation Rating** worksheet.

> ☞ *You may want to provide taped copies of your narration for members to practice with at home. On the last page of this manual, you will find a list of relaxation audiotapes.*

## Participant Preparation

Pages 29–45 of *Overcoming Panic, Anxiety, & Phobias* will help participants prepare for this session and will reinforce what they learn during the session.

## Process

1. Introduce the exercise by making the following comments:

©1996 Whole Person Press 210 W Michigan Duluth MN 55802     (800) 247-6789

- When you feel anxious, your muscles respond by becoming tense, and your breathing becomes shallow.

- You may not even recognize the tension in your body, but it increases your anxiety and brings on other uncomfortable physical sensations.

- By reducing this physical tension, you can keep your anxiety from escalating and can actually reduce it.

- Today, you will begin to learn the beneficial effects of relaxation. Some people will experience anxiety when first practicing relaxation exercises. If this happens to you, I encourage you to continue the exercise in order to use this reaction to gain evidence that these sensations are uncomfortable but harmless.

2. Distribute the **Tension/Relaxation Rating** worksheet and provide the following instructions:

➤ Enter today's date in column one of the worksheet.

➤ Take a moment to rate, on a scale from 1 to 10, your present level of anxiety. Record that figure in column two.

➤ In the fourth column, list the events, thoughts, and physical sensations that have contributed to your feelings of stress or anxiety.

➤ Now set the worksheet aside.

3. If music is available, begin playing it softly, then, speaking slowly and quietly, introduce the relaxation exercise by making the following comments:

- Now we will take several minutes to relax our bodies and our minds by alternately tightening and relaxing different muscle groups.

- First, make yourself comfortable. Adjust any part of your clothing that feels uncomfortable. If you wish, take off your shoes. If you're wearing glasses, you may wish to remove them.

- Now close your eyes, if that feels comfortable to you.

■ When I ask you to tighten your muscles, do it firmly enough so you notice the tension but not to a degree where the tightness could cause distress later.

■ As we proceed, remember to breathe gently and slowly. When you release your tightened muscles, you can help them relax by slowly exhaling at the same time. Hold the tension for at least 5 seconds, then relax for 15–30 seconds while exhaling.

4. Begin reading the relaxation script very slowly and quietly, pausing after each phrase.

*Make a fist in front of you, holding your arm out straight . . . feeling the tension in your fist and forearm. Notice the tension . . . hold it . . . and then relax and lower your arm, allowing your arm to fall gently to your side. Notice any difference as your arm begins to let go of tension.*

*Now wrinkle your forehead, trying to bring your eyebrows up to your scalp, noticing the tension at the tip of your nose and over each eyebrow . . . hold it . . . and then release the muscles, concentrating on any difference as you allow yourself to feel some relaxation in this area of your body.*

*Next, make a face, squeezing all of your facial muscles as tightly as you can. Close your eyes tightly and make a smile, tightening all your cheek muscles, hold it . . . hold it . . . and then let go of the tension. Focus on the sensation of relaxation and what that is like for you as you allow your muscles to relax further and further, under your control.*

*Clench your teeth as hard as you can without causing pain. Push your tongue up against the roof of your mouth. Now relax your jaw and tongue, and think about enjoying the sensation of letting go.*

*Tighten your neck and shoulders, bringing your shoulders up toward your ears. Pay special attention to the areas where you feel tense, especially the back and sides of your neck . . . now let go as much as you possibly can, letting your*

*shoulders droop. Then let go a little more. Focus on the
sensations in your shoulders and neck. You may feel as if
you've had a nice soothing massage. Tighten your stomach
muscles, hold the tension . . . and then let it go . . . noticing
any difference.*

*Take a slow, gentle breath. Then take another one—slowly
in through your nose and slowly out through your mouth.
Raise your leg. Turn your toes up and back and make your
whole leg rigid . . . feel the tension, notice what it feels like.
Then slowly relax and lower your leg. Notice the difference
between the tension and relaxation.*

*Bring your fists up high on your chest, pull them back and
clench them as hard as you can. Notice how your shoulders
and back feel, notice the tension. Now slowly open your hands
and let your arms fall naturally to your side, noticing the
difference in how your shoulders, back, and arms feel.*

*Now tighten all the muscles in your calves and thighs, one
leg at a time. First, make your left leg rigid and hold
it . . . hold it . . . let the tension go. Then make your right leg
rigid . . . hold it . . . hold it. You can feel yourself rise off the
chair a little. Notice where the tension is, especially in the
tops and bottoms of your thighs . . . and now let the tension
go. Feel the relaxation in every part of your legs . . . your
thighs . . . your knees . . . your calves . . . your
ankles . . . your feet . . . your toes.*

*Continue to notice the relaxation in your legs as you
breathe very slowly and gently to a count of 6, pausing
between the inhale and exhale for a second . . . .in . . . and
out . . . in . . . and out . . . (pause for 30 seconds).*

*You have now given relaxing attention to every part of
your body. As you continue to breathe slowly and gently, take
a few moments to scan your body and let go of any tension
that remains. Use the technique we've just used. First, tense
the muscles in that area, and then, as you slowly exhale, let*

*go of the tension (pause for 1–2 minutes).*

   *When you are ready, open your eyes. Take a minute to just feel your breath and look around the room, holding on to those feelings of deep relaxation (pause for 1 minute).*

5. Give the following instructions:

➤ Now, before we start talking with each other again, please take the **Tension/Relaxation Rating** worksheet and enter your current tension rating in the third column, "After the exercise."

➤ Use this worksheet at home. Rating your tension prior to and after practicing progressive muscle relaxation will help you recognize the changes you are able to bring about through relaxation techniques. Practice one or more times each day.

6. Encourage participants to continue practicing these techniques.

■ As you continue to practice relaxation techniques, you will find that it becomes easier and quicker for you to fully relax. You will then be ready to use these techniques to increase your ability to manage stressful situations.

■ To relax on cue, focus your attention on any tension in your body. Begin your calm, centered breathing. Say "inhale" to yourself on each inhale. With each exhale, say "relax" to yourself and focus on releasing tension from your body. Use this relaxation technique throughout the day—at work, while driving, during social gatherings, at home, while shopping.

©1996 Whole Person Press 210 W Michigan Duluth MN 55802     (800) 247-6789

## TENSION/RELAXATION RATING

Rate your feelings before and after the relaxation exercise from 1 (most relaxed) to 10 (most tense).

| Date | Before the exercise | After the exercise | List the events, thoughts, and physical sensations that had contributed to your feelings of stress. |
|---|---|---|---|
| | | | |

©1996 Whole Person Press 210 W Michigan Duluth MN 55802     (800) 247-6789

# Feeling the Breath

Participants use calm, centered breathing to relax.

## Goal

To learn and experience the most advantageous kind of breathing for promoting relaxation and mental calm.

## Group Size

Unlimited.

## Time

10 minutes.

## Materials

None.

## Participant Preparation

Pages 29–31, 37–39 of *Overcoming Panic, Anxiety, & Phobias* will help participants prepare for this session and will reinforce what they learn during the session.

## Process

1. Introduce the benefits of calm, centered breathing with the following comments:

   ■ Recovery from anxiety and panic begins with body awareness, and body awareness begins with awareness of our breathing. During anxious moments or panic attacks, if you experience heart palpitations, dizziness, blurred vision, or other scary physical sensations, you may be hyperventilating. Once you become aware of overbreathing–rapid or forced breathing–– you can use the breath to calm your body and your mind.

   ■ Today, we are going to practice the kind of calm breathing that you can use any time, any place, to calm yourself and help yourself stay in the present.

2. Help participants prepare themselves by giving the following instructions:

➤ First, make yourself comfortable. Adjust any part of your clothing that feels uncomfortable. If you wish, take off your shoes. If you're wearing glasses, you may wish to remove them.

➤ Now close your eyes, if that feels comfortable to you.

3. Begin reading the relaxation script very slowly and quietly, pausing after each phrase.

*Take a slow, gentle breath in through your nose. Hold it for a second . . . and then slowly breathe out through your mouth, pursing your lips as if you are sipping through a straw.*

*You can use counting to focus your attention and slow down your breathing. In a moment, while I count, try inhaling to a count of six, holding for a count of three, and exhaling to a count of six.*

*Inhale, 2, 3, 4, 5, 6; hold, 2, 3; exhale slowly, 2, 3, 4, 5, 6. Let's repeat. Inhale, 2, 3, 4, 5, 6; hold, 2, 3; exhale, 2, 3, 4, 5, 6. Continue breathing in this slow, gentle manner as I talk for a few moments.*

*In time, as you get more used to slow, gentle breathing, you may want to breathe even more slowly, especially on the exhalation. You'll soon notice that your body knows how long it wants to take for each phase of breathing. Continue to use the breath to focus your attention and calm your body and mind. As you gently practice, the benefits of this calm, centered breathing will occur.*

*Remember to keep on breathing slowly and gently. Inhale, 2, 3, 4, 5, 6; hold, 2, 3; exhale slowly, 2, 3, 4, 5, 6. Let's repeat. Inhale, 2, 3, 4, 5, 6; hold, 2, 3; exhale, 2, 3, 4, 5, 6. Continue breathing slowly and gently as I talk.*

*The diaphragm, the large muscle at the bottom of the rib cage, controls breathing. When it contracts, it creates more space in the chest cavity, which causes the lungs to expand. If your belly is relaxed, this movement will cause it to move outward slightly as you inhale and back in as you exhale. Put your hand on your stomach, about where your belt buckle would be, and watch your hand gently rise and fall as you breathe. If you've ever watched a baby or an animal breathe, you've seen this gentle movement of the abdomen.*

*Remember to breathe slowly. I'll count again for you: 1, 2, 3, 4, 5, 6; hold, 2, 3; out, 2, 3, 4, 5, 6. Good.*

*Many of us have learned to keep our abdominal muscles tightened; but relaxed breathing works better when we relax these muscles. You may have to try this for awhile before it starts to feel comfortable.*

*When you are ready, open your eyes. Take a minute to just feel your breath and look around the room, becoming aware of whatever you are experiencing at this moment (pause for 1 minute).*

4. Conclude the session by making the following comments:

   ■ Breathing in this slow, calming way can make your symptoms of anxiety less severe and can actually lower your anxiety level.

   ■ Try practicing at home once or twice a day.

   ■ As you continue to practice calm, centered breathing, you will find that it becomes easier and quicker for you to release tension. You will then be ready to use this technique to reduce the intensity or number of your anxiety or panic attacks.

# Calming Cue Words and Images

Participants develop a list of relaxing words and images.

## Goals

To help participants understand the value of relaxation.

To give participants a variety of words and images they can use to help them relax during stressful times.

## Group Size

Unlimited.

## Time

30 minutes.

## Materials

Pencils; 3 "x 5 "index cards; easel and easel paper; markers.

## Participant Preparation

Pages 35–40 of *Overcoming Panic, Anxiety, & Phobias* will help participants prepare for this session and will reinforce what they learn during the session.

## Process

1. Introduce the exercise with the following comments:

   ■ The power of suggestion is greater than you might think. Your mind and your body can respond dramatically to simple words and images.

   ■ Here's an example of how quickly the power of suggestion can work:

   *Close your eyes and imagine that you are holding in your hands a bright yellow lemon and a paring knife. As you cut the lemon in half, watch the juice spurt from it. Now take one of the juicy lemon halves and bring it to your mouth. Lick the tart flesh, then slowly squeeze the juice into your mouth. When you've drunk it all, open your eyes.*

▪ If you are like most people, your salivary glands have now become as active just thinking about the lemon as if you had actually eaten it.

2. Write the word "excitement" on the easel paper. Continue to develop the idea of cue words and images that evoke physical sensations and emotions by asking participants the following questions, noting their responses on the easel paper:

✔ I'd like you to think about the word "excitement." Some people feel excited when they think about a roller coaster. What are some images that make you feel excited?

✔ If you were sitting quietly, what words might make you feel excited?

3. On a clean piece of easel paper, write the word "relaxation," and make the following comments about the value of relaxation in reducing stress.

▪ If you are suffering from anxiety or panic, you probably have enough excitement in your life, although it may be that your own body is providing it.

▪ The ability to relax quickly and easily can mute your body's response to anxious thoughts and make it possible for you to think rationally about your fears and to deliberately confront anxiety-producing situations and body sensations.

▪ You can learn to respond to relaxation cues as easily as you did to the thought of a lemon.

4. Continue by giving the following instructions:

*Close your eyes again. Begin breathing slowly and smoothly to a count of 6 . . . inhale . . . and exhale . . . slowly and deeply.*

*Imagine yourself in a place of quiet and calm: a sunlit beach, a forest glen, wherever you find tranquility. When you have the image clear in your mind, keep your eyes closed as you take turns describing your peaceful place to me. I'll make a few notes on the easel paper.*

5. When all participants have described their images, ask them to open their eyes, then take a few minutes to discuss the likenesses and differences they see in the images listed on the easel paper.

6. Advise participants that although imagery is a wonderful way to induce the physical and emotional benefits of relaxation, it is possible to train their bodies to relax virtually on command. Continue with the following instructions:

   ➤ I'd like you to list as many words as possible that are calming and relaxing. Let's start with the word "calm"; I'll put it at the top of the list. Please continue listing words that seem relaxing to you.

   ➤ Now that the paper is covered with words, select the word that seems most relaxing to you.

   ➤ Close your eyes again and make yourself comfortable. Begin breathing slowly . . . and evenly . . . slowly . . . and evenly. Each time you exhale, quietly breathe out your calming word. Inhale . . . and exhale your word. Inhale . . . and exhale your word.

7. After 2–3 minutes, ask participants to open their eyes and process their experience with the group. Encourage them to practice several times a day with their relaxing image and their calming word. Regular practice will make it possible for them to induce relaxation quickly by merely recalling the image or saying the word.

8. Suggest that they record their favorite images and calming words on index cards or in their journals. Encourage participants to refer to their calming words whenever they feel anxious.

# Mindful Meditation

Participants are taught and practice mindful meditation during which they focus on their breath and allow themselves to return to their breathing when they become aware of thoughts.

## Goals

To experience mindfulness, the attitude at the heart of meditation and to learn techniques for managing anxiety.

To acquire a technique that can be used, any time, any place, to calm the mind and body.

To learn to observe anxiety reactions in a more detached manner.

## Group Size

Unlimited.

## Time

20 minutes.

## Materials

None.

## Participant Preparation

Pages 35–41 of *Overcoming Panic, Anxiety, & Phobias* will help participants prepare for this session and will reinforce what they learn during the session.

## Process

1. Introduce the exercise with a few comments on the benefits of being present in each moment rather than dwelling on the past or fearing the future.

2. Suggest to participants that for the next 10 minutes they will be practicing "mindful meditation." Instruct the group to focus on

their breathing and when they become aware of their thoughts, without judging, to refocus on their breathing. Read the script that follows, speaking softly and slowly and pausing between sentences.

*Make yourself comfortable . . . closing your eyes if you wish. If you want to leave your eyes open, focus on some spot in the room. Allow yourself to bring your attention to your breathing, taking a breath and noticing your breath as it moves in and out of your body . . . take another breath . . . hold it . . . and let it go. Continue to focus your attention on your breath as it passes in . . . and out . . . again and again . . . it doesn't matter whether the breathing happens in a certain way. Without any effort, your breathing will be okay . . . your body knows how much air it needs . . . so just begin to observe the in-breath . . . and the out-breath . . . all you need to do is to continue to focus on your breath . . . When thoughts come in, notice them floating like twigs in a stream and passing away . . . no need to judge . . . just observe . . . and when you become aware of your thoughts, just gently bring your attention back to your breath. Notice your breath as it goes in and out . . . Notice any difference in the breathing, without trying to control it . . . Focus on the current breath . . . If your thoughts wander, as they will . . . gently bring your attention back to the breathing, noting what that is like for you . . . allow your breathing to become slower . . . Notice your body in the chair . . . how you are sitting . . . what your body feels like . . . the sounds and smells around you . . . As you notice things going on outside you and within you, do so without evaluating or trying to control . . . Now gently bring your thoughts back to your breath, allowing yourself to be fully in this moment . . . There is no right or wrong way to meditate. Observe your thoughts as if they were on a stream, traveling down the water . . . just note the thoughts without rejecting or pursuing them. Just observe and let them go . . . observe and let them go . . . and*

*then bring your attention back to the breath . . . If you begin
to judge or try to control, notice what that does to your
breathing . . . then simply resume your focus on the
breath . . . using the breath as a point from which to observe
thoughts which will inevitably come to mind . . . the urges,
planning, memories, impatience which hinder our ability to
just be in this moment . . . adopt a nonjudgmental attitude of
acceptance . . . and when you become aware of these thoughts
just allow yourself to be with your breath . . . Remember,
there is no right or wrong way to meditate. Whenever your
mind wanders, gently bring it back to the breath, just observing the process . . . just refocusing on the breath without
judging . . . When you gain awareness of judging or impatience or trying to control, observe the process and then bring
your attention back to your breath. Just bring your mind back
to the breath when it wanders, knowing that it may wander
hundreds of times . . . and each time return to the breath
without judging.*

*When you feel ready, begin to gradually bring yourself
back to the room . . . stretch your body . . . gain a sense of the
room . . . and then, slowly open your eyes . . . knowing that in
time you can bring on this state of appreciating and being in
the moment, observing your thoughts instead of getting stuck
in them . . . developing a detachment from your excess
anxiety throughout the day.*

☞ *If someone becomes distressed during this exercise, let them
practice gentle breathing or progressive muscle relaxation
instead. A permissive attitude is desirable. People with severe
personality disorders or psychological problems may not be
appropriate candidates for meditation.*

3. Conclude the session by asking participants to describe their
   experience. Some participants will find the exercise relaxing,
   others will have been tense, anxious, or restless. Stress that all
   these reactions are OK, making the following comments:

---

- People experience a variety of sensations during meditation. Many people find these sensations to be comfortable. Others feel somewhat uncomfortable.

- However, daily practice can help you become adept at being in the present, observing your reactions and becoming less fearful of whatever occurs. You will learn to adopt an observant attitude toward your thoughts and physical sensations.

- In time you can start using mindful meditation by taking a "mini-meditation break" during stressful episodes. Observe the effect on your anxiety level as you learn to observe scary thoughts without needing to react to them or fear them, instead bringing your attention back to your breath.

# Getting to the Heart of the Matter

Use this exercise to introduce participants to a new way of thinking about their problems. The session should be led by a mental health professional.

## Goals

To introduce participants to a rational approach to their problems.

To prepare participants to challenge all their beliefs, including basic assumptions about themselves.

## Group Size

Unlimited.

## Time

1–2 hours.

## Materials

Pencils; **Getting to the Heart of the Matter** worksheet.

## Participant Preparation

Pages 49–52 of *Overcoming Panic, Anxiety, & Phobias* will help participants prepare for this session and will reinforce what they learn during the session.

> ☞ *Be prepared for the anxiety that may be brought to the surface during this exercise. Some of the participant's most feared peril predictions can be quite catastrophic.*

## Process

1. Lead a discussion of the Frightened You and the Rational You, pausing to ask for discussion after you make each point.

   ■ You probably think of yourself as a rational being; that's part of what it means to be human. When you are in the throes of a panic attack or anxiety episode, however, distressing physical sensations and terrifying emotions can overwhelm the Rational You, leaving the Frightened You in control. Describe a time when you had this type of experience.

■ When the Frightened You is in command during an anxiety episode, you give yourself catastrophic messages about your situation. If you are experiencing excess anxiety, you are probably worrying about a future event; during a panic attack, you probably fear an immediate peril. Describe the kind of dire predictions you make when you are extremely anxious or in the midst of a panic attack.

■ As a group, we're going to look at how peril predictions can escalate to irrational fear.

2. Prepare a sample **Getting to the Heart of the Matter** worksheet on easel paper Ask the following questions and, as participants respond, begin filling out the worksheet:

✔ What fears might an anxious person have?

☞ *As participants call out responses, select an appropriate one and record it on the easel paper.*

✔ Since peril predictions often escalate, ask yourself some questions that an anxious person might be unconsciously asking, for instance:

If that event were to occur, what might happen next?

And what would be so terrible about that?

☞ *Repeatedly ask the two questions listed above, attempting after several rounds of questions to elicit all the frightening predictions that underlie the initial peril prediction.*

3. Continue the discussion making the following points:

■ You can give yourself a lot of frightening peril predictions. You may not be familiar with looking beyond your urge to flee, avoid, check repeatedly, or procrastinate. You may not wish to focus on all the consequences of your predictions about what might happen next and the frightening consequences that could follow. However, it is possible to collect all your peril predictions and begin to think more rationally about the actual likelihood of them happening and your ability to cope if they did.

■ Before you experiment with allowing the Rational You to help you face your fears, it's essential to consider exactly what all your fears are and to look at how they can escalate.

4. Distribute the **Getting to the Heart of the Matter** worksheet and give the following instructions:

➤ On this worksheet, list one of your peril predictions—a fear that seems to precipitate your excess anxiety or panic attacks.

➤ Just as we did on the easel paper, record on your worksheet what you fear might happen next, and what would be so bad if that event did happen.

➤ Continue to ask yourself those questions and record your answers until you believe you have uncovered all your fears.

➤ As you complete the worksheet, you may find yourself becoming somewhat anxious. This is quite normal and is actually an opportunity for you to experience, in a safe environment with people who understand, some of the physical sensations that accompany your anxiety or panic attacks. You can begin to realize that, although you are uncomfortable, these scary sensations do not actually predict that anything bad will happen.

5. After participants have completed their worksheets, ask them to share any insights they gained during the activity. Encourage them to express their emotions, but remind them to allow the Rational You to evaluate their peril predictions.

6. Conclude the exercise by reminding participants that as they continue on the journey toward recovery they will become better at identifying all of their peril predictions and learning how to challenge them.

# GETTING TO THE HEART OF THE MATTER

My peril prediction _____

_____

_____

_____

| If that occurs, what might happen next? | What would be so bad about that? |
|---|---|
| If that occurs, what might happen next? | What would be so bad about that? |
| If that occurs, what might happen next? | What would be so bad about that? |
| If that occurs, what might happen next? | What would be so bad about that? |

# My Security Moves

In this simple exercise, participants focus on the security moves that may temporarily lower their anxiety but that ultimately reinforce their fears. This exercise should be led by a mental health professional.

## Goals

To focus on the often unnecessary things that people with anxiety problems do to feel secure, actions they take that may play a part in maintaining their fears.

To recognize, rethink, and eliminate unnecessary security moves.

## Group Size

6–10.

## Time

1–2 hours.

## Materials

Easel and easel paper; markers; **My Security Moves** worksheet.

## Participant Preparation

Pages 75–80 of *Overcoming Panic, Anxiety, & Phobias* will help participants prepare for this session and will reinforce what they learn during the session.

## Process

1. Help participants understand what security moves are by making the following comments:
   - Every day you take many actions to keep yourself safe. You buckle your seat belt. You look both ways before crossing the street. You keep electrical appliances away from water. You avoid vicious dogs. These actions are reasonable and prudent.

- If, however, you are troubled by anxious thoughts, you may increase the number and variety of strategies you use to keep safe. If, for instance, you become anxious in the presence of dogs, you may go to great lengths to avoid coming in contact with them. You may decide that only one street or time of day is safe for a walk, or you may feel you need someone with you at all times in case a dog appears. Or you may feel you need to check the papers over and over for any reports of dog-related injuries. You may reduce your current fear but at the cost of reducing your freedom in the future.

- If you feel worried about socializing at a party, you may try to avoid uncomfortable feelings by distracting yourself from your anxious thoughts with an unrelated activity or by having a few drinks before you leave for the party.

- These self-protective behaviors are called security moves. What's good about them is that they work; they do reduce your anxiety to some degree. Unfortunately, the relief is temporary because the fear remains.

- When you use security moves, you reinforce your sense that there really is something to be feared, something that you are warding off with these protective behaviors. Security moves can become part of the problem rather than part of the solution if they keep you from confronting your anxiety and finding effective methods of dealing with it.

- You may have difficulty identifying your security moves; they often are subtle and unconscious. If you do have trouble determining which of your behaviors are security moves, ask yourself what stopped your peril prediction from happening the last time you experienced excess anxiety or panic.

2. Distribute the **My Security Moves** worksheet and tell participants that they should list in the appropriate column their security moves—the ways in which they protect themselves from situations, physical sensations, and thoughts that they fear. Allow 5 minutes for them to do this.

---

3. While participants are working on their individual worksheets, prepare a blank worksheet on the easel paper.

4. Through group discussion and brainstorming, help participants understand how to begin challenging and eliminating their security moves. Give participants the following instructions:

➤ One at a time, I'd like each of you to mention one of your security moves. I'll list them on the easel paper.

➤ Now, help each other by looking at each security move and brainstorming ways to challenge these security moves, ways to face anxiety-producing situations without these self-protective behaviors.

> ☞ *As participants offer ideas, write them on the easel paper in the column headed "Challenge strategy."*

➤ Look at the column headed "Benefits for the future." Take a few minutes to consider the security move that you contributed to our list. Consider the benefits that will come to you when you can face your fear directly. As you come up with ideas, state them out loud and I'll add them to our chart.

5. Conclude the session with the following comments:

■ Today, we've looked at the benefits and risks of protecting yourself from anxiety with security moves. You shared ideas about how to challenge those moves and looked at some of the benefits that will come from eliminating them.

■ Only one column on our easel worksheet is empty—the column labeled "What happened?" During the next week, I'd like you to complete the columns labeled "Challenge strategy" and "Benefits for the future" on your own worksheet.

■ Then begin with the security move that you think will be easiest to eliminate. Try challenging it, then record the result in the "What happened?" column. You may find that the increase in anxiety that comes when first facing your fear directly is compensated for by the benefits you receive, including your new confidence. And as you continue to challenge your security moves, your anxiety level will lower as you gain evidence that what you fear doesn't occur or is not as big a catastrophe as you thought it would be.

■ When you have successfully eliminated one security move, continue with another. When all your security moves have been eliminated, you'll be well on the way to recovery.

## Variations

■ Allow participants to work in teams of two, each interviewing the other and presenting the other's security moves to the group.

■ Develop a continuing list of security moves for the entire group. Add to it each week as more are identified.

| MY SECURITY MOVES | | | |
|---|---|---|---|
| Security move | Challenge strategy | What happened? | Benefits for the future |
| | | | |

# Strengthening the Rational You

This exercise helps participants systematically track their anxious thought processes by describing their anxious peril predictions and putting them in context. The session should be led by a mental health professional.

## Goals

To introduce participants to a rational approach to their problems.

To reinforce each participant's sense that it is possible to move beyond their worry and to think their way through the situation.

## Group Size

6–10.

## Time

1–2 hours.

## Materials

Pencils; easel and easel paper; markers; **Looking at the Odds: Strengthening the Rational You** worksheet; **Looking at the Danger: Strengthening the Rational You** worksheet.

## Participant Preparation

Pages 47–66 of *Overcoming Panic, Anxiety, & Phobias* will help participants prepare for this session and will reinforce what they learn during the session.

## Part 1: Looking at the odds

## Process

1. Present a 10–15 minute overview of this basic cognitive therapy technique and its benefits to people who are anxious:

- People who suffer from anxiety problems often appear to have two distortions in their thinking:

  They overestimate the probability that whatever concerns them and causes them anxiety will occur.

  They catastrophize, overestimating the severity of the potential consequences if the peril prediction does occur.

- Overestimating and catastrophizing are two ways of thinking that can keep you trapped within your anxiety or panic cycle.

- Today we are going to begin using one of the key strategies in cognitive therapy, a strategy that will challenge your tendency to overestimate danger and to catastrophize about consequences. In this process, you will examine your thoughts and begin to question your conclusions about the danger you have been perceiving.

- Sometimes people think cognitive therapy is about thinking positive thoughts. It would be great if you could just say, "There's nothing to be worried about," and then relax. But, as you know, this doesn't work all the time.

- Rather than spend time on the easy but ineffective process of positive thinking, you will engage in a more difficult but far more effective process. Instead of ignoring the frightening messages you are giving yourself, you will begin to focus on them and to think clearly about the evidence for and against these messages.

- You will be well along your way to recovery from panic and anxiety when you can weigh the evidence for your predictions and develop more realistic interpretations of this evidence.

- In order to really believe these less frightening predictions, you will need to expose yourself to what you have been afraid of. That's the only way you can test your new beliefs.

- The new beliefs come from the Rational You. However, the Frightened You has had a strong hold on you. It's been keeping you a prisoner, and it will take a lot of experimentation for you to truly believe any new information you give yourself.

©1996 Whole Person Press 210 W Michigan Duluth MN 55802     (800) 247-6789

▓ The exercises that you engage in today will help you gain new information. You will learn how to systematically test your thinking and how to let go of thoughts that have been keeping you trapped. First, you have to learn some new ways to assess the thoughts you are experiencing.

2. Distribute the **Looking at the Odds: Strengthening the Rational You** worksheet and present the following instructions, pausing to allow participants to ask questions and to complete each step before moving on to the next:

☞ *Participants are probably unfamiliar with the concepts of anxiety cues and peril predictions. Present an example from Overcoming Panic, Anxiety, & Phobias on easel paper.*

➤ Think back over the past week and recall a time in which you felt overly anxious or experienced a panic attack. If you can't remember any event from the past week, select an event occurring earlier. Record this date in the first section of the worksheet.

➤ In the second section of the worksheet, fill in your anxiety cues. These are the events, thoughts, or physical sensations that triggered your anxiety or panic. The sensations you experience during an anxiety episode can be so distressing that you may be unaware of any specific cues. It may seem that the anxiety just floods over you. For you to become fully aware of the cues that trigger your anxiety will take time and practice. Do the best you can right now.

➤ Record in the third section what your peril prediction was. This peril prediction came from the Frightened You. If it's hard to recall your specific fear, imagine yourself back in the anxiety-producing situation. Relive it as if you were watching a movie, then write down what you were afraid would happen.

➤ In the fourth section of your worksheet, estimate on a scale from 0 to 100 percent the likelihood of this peril prediction occurring—not the way you feel now but the way you felt when you were in the midst of the anxiety or panic episode.

3. After everyone has filled out the first four sections of the worksheet, ask for a volunteer who is willing to share a peril prediction and anxiety cues. As you work through the following questions with this volunteer, record the answers on a facsimile of the worksheet that you have prepared on easel paper. Allow time for participants to ask questions and discuss their reactions to the questions and answers.

   ✔ What were the anxiety cues: the events, thoughts, or physical sensations that triggered your anxiety?

   ✔ What was your peril prediction; what did you fear would happen?

   ✔ On a scale from 0 to 100 percent, how likely did it seem, during your anxiety or panic episode, that your peril prediction would occur?

4. Continue the process by asking participants to complete all but the last section of their worksheet. Give time after each instruction for them to ask questions and to respond in writing.

   ➤ Now that you have identified your peril prediction, I'd like you to look for specific evidence for and against the likelihood of your peril prediction occurring. Begin by recording all the evidence you can in support of your peril prediction occurring.

   ➤ Next, think of all the evidence against your peril prediction occurring and record that information.

   ➤ And finally, after looking at all the evidence, on a scale from 0 to 100 percent, how likely does it now seem that your peril prediction will occur?

5. After participants are done writing, continue by asking questions of the original volunteer, again allowing time for questions and discussion.

   ✔ You've filled in your form. What evidence have you put down for and against your prediction?

   ✔ After reviewing all the evidence from the Rational You, what was your new rating for the probability of your prediction happening?

6. Conclude this part of the exercise by giving instructions for completion of the last section of the worksheet:

➤ In the last section of your worksheet, write some new statements based on your review of all the evidence that you can give yourself when you begin to feel or worry about excess anxiety or panic.

➤ Record these messages on a 3 " x 5 " index card and carry it with you. Read them at any time, but especially when you are feeling anxious. They will strengthen the Rational You.

## Part 2: Looking at the danger

### Process

1. You have looked at the probability of your peril prediction occurring. Now I'd like you to look at just how bad it would be if your worst fear happened.

▪ The danger that you are predicting could have major or minimal consequences. If you are predicting you will have a heart attack and die, that certainly would be a catastrophe.

▪ On the other hand, some consequences may involve uncomfortable feelings or momentary embarrassment rather than disaster. You've already considered how likely it is that the worst will happen; it's equally important that you become clear about how bad it would really be if the worst does happen.

2. Distribute the **Looking at the Danger: Strengthening the Rational You** worksheet and present the following instructions, pausing to allow participants to ask questions and to complete each step before moving on to the next:

➤ In the first three sections of your worksheet, copy your anxiety cues and peril predictions from your previous worksheet.

➤ In the fourth section of your worksheet, estimate on a scale from 0 to 100 percent the seriousness of the consequences if this peril prediction occurs—not the way you feel now but the way you felt when you were in the midst of the anxiety or panic episode.

3. After everyone has filled out the first four sections of the worksheet, ask for a new volunteer who is willing to share a peril prediction and anxiety cues. As you work through the following questions with this volunteer, record the answers on a facsimile of the worksheet that you have prepared on easel paper. Allow time for participants to ask questions and discuss their reactions to the questions and answers.

✔ What were the anxiety cues: the events, thoughts, or physical sensations that triggered your anxiety?

✔ What was your peril prediction; what did you fear would happen?

✔ On a scale from 0 to 100 percent, how serious did the consequences seem during your anxiety or panic episode, if your peril prediction had occurred?

4. Continue the process by asking participants to complete all but the last section of their worksheet. Give time after each instruction for them to ask questions and to respond in writing.

➤ I'd like you to look for specific evidence for and against the seriousness of the consequences if your peril prediction occurs.

➤ Begin by recording all the evidence you can think of why the consequences would be catastrophic if your peril prediction occurs.

➤ Next, record all the evidence against tragic consequences if your peril prediction occurs. Be sure to consider the fact that you may be able to cope with the peril you are predicting and that you might do have the ability to recover in time.

➤ And finally, after looking at all the evidence, on a scale from

0 to 100 percent, how serious will the consequences be if your peril prediction occurs?

5. After participants are done writing, continue by asking questions of your volunteer, again allowing time for questions and discussion.

   ✔ You've filled in your form. What evidence have you put down for and against catastrophic consequences if your peril prediction occurs?

   ✔ After reviewing all the evidence from the Rational You, what was your new rating for the seriousness of these consequences?

6. Conclude this part of the exercise by giving instructions for completion of the last section of the worksheet:

   ➤ In the last section of your worksheet, write some supportive messages that you can give yourself when you begin to feel anxious or panicked. These messages should be based on your review of the evidence.

   ➤ Record these messages on a 3 " x 5 " index card and carry it with you. Read them at any time, but especially when you begin to worry about the danger involved in your peril prediction. They will strengthen the Rational You.

7. Conclude the exercise by leading a discussion about these two worksheets and the conclusions participants have come to. Encourage participants to adopt a problem-solving approach, to offer specific solutions, and to help each other.

# LOOKING AT THE ODDS:
## STRENGTHENING THE RATIONAL YOU

a. Day/time:

b. Anxiety cue (events/thoughts/sensations):

c. My peril prediction:

d. Odds that my peril prediction will occur (0–100%):

e. Evidence for the likelihood of my peril prediction occurring:

f. Evidence against the likelihood of my peril prediction occurring:

g. New odds that my peril prediction will occur (0–100%):

h. New self-talk after reviewing all the evidence:

## LOOKING AT THE DANGER:
## STRENGTHENING THE RATIONAL YOU

a. Day/time:

b. Anxiety cues (events/thoughts/sensations):

c. My peril prediction:

d. Danger severity rating (0–100%):

e. Evidence for catastrophe if my peril prediction happens:

f. Evidence against catastrophe if my peril prediction happens:

g. New danger severity rating (0–100%):

h. New self-talk after reviewing all the evidence:

# Am I Perfect Enough?

This exercise addresses the perfectionism, the need to control, and the desire to please that are characteristic of many people with severe anxiety.

## Goals

To introduce the idea that people have options in the ways they behave.

To chip away, using humor, at ingrained assumptions that get in the way of a satisfying life.

## Group Size

Unlimited.

## Time

1 hour.

## Materials

Pencils; paper.

## Participant Preparation

Pages 66–74 of *Overcoming Panic, Anxiety, & Phobias* will help participants prepare for this session and will reinforce what they learn during the session.

## Process

☞ *Write the following words in a column on the easel paper: perfectionism, control, people pleasing, competence, responsibility, dependence, and undesirability.*

1. Introduce the topic with the following comments:

   ▪ Many of your thoughts spring from basic beliefs that you have about yourself and others.

■ These beliefs usually develop in childhood. For example, if someone said you were clumsy because you tumbled over a toy, you may have believed it, and you may still believe it.

■ Unfortunately, these beliefs become ingrained and hard to challenge when you are an adult even when all the evidence shows your basic belief to be untrue.

■ Today, I'd like you to take a good look at some of the assumptions that may be robbing your life of joy and freedom.

2. Give participants the following instructions:

➤ I'm going to read a series of sentences that are related to the words on the easel paper.

➤ If a sentence expresses your feelings about yourself, raise your hand. I'll count the raised hands and record the number after the appropriate word.

➤ After all the sentences have been read, we'll add the numbers and, in that way, determine which kinds of assumptions are most troublesome to the members of this group.

3. Begin reading the sentences aloud and counting raised hands. After each of the seven words on the easel paper, you should record four numbers, one number for each sentence.

■ Perfectionism
I feel a constant pressure to achieve.
I criticize myself when my performance isn't perfect.
I rarely feel I've done enough no matter how hard I try.
I often give up pleasure in order to be the best at everything
   I do.

■ Control
I have to be perfectly in control at all times.
I worry about how I appear to others when I am feeling
   anxious.
I feel that any lack of control is a sign of weakness or failure.
I don't feel safe if I allow someone else to take control of a
   situation.

▪ People pleasing
  My self-esteem depends on everyone else's opinion of me.
  I will do things I'd rather not do so others will like me.
  I am better at caring for others than caring for myself.
  I keep most of my negative feelings inside to avoid displeasing
    others.

▪ Competence
  I believe that I can never do as good a job as other people.
  I believe that my judgment is poor.
  I believe that I lack common sense.
  I feel like an imposter when I am told my work is good.

▪ Responsibility
  I must always be there for others.
  No matter how stressed and overloaded I feel, I have to do
    whatever I am asked.
  I shouldn't ask for help no matter how much I need it.
  I have to fulfill the needs of other people before I take care of
    myself.

▪ Dependence
  I feel unable to manage on my own.
  I need to have people help me or be around when I'm anxious.
  I need a lot of reassurance from others.
  I see myself as a dependent and helpless person.

▪ Undesirability
  If people knew how uncomfortable I feel, they would not
    want to be with me.
  I'm unattractive and turn people off.
  I'm uninteresting and have nothing to say.
  If anyone sees any sign of my anxiety, they'll know how
    defective I really am.

4. Add the numbers written after each word on the easel paper,
   then ask participants to comment on the areas that are of
   concern to most of them. If they need help in recalling the
   sentences, it may be necessary to reread them.

5. Give participants time to write in their journals about the way some or all of these characteristics apply to them.

6. Ask participants to form into groups of three or four. Distribute paper and give the following instructions:

   ➤ Brainstorm ways, for example, in which you can fight your tendency to strive for perfection and to please everybody. Try to cover the paper with a multitude of imaginative ideas. I will give you 10 minutes to complete this process.

   ➤ Now develop a scenario in which you will act in a way that will test one of your basic beliefs. For example, if you check your work many times in order to be perfect, check half as much, allow yourself to feel the anxiety, and then review the consequences.

7. Reassemble the entire group and ask participants to report on their plans. Encourage support for everyone's effort.

8. Encourage participants to support their buddies or members of their small groups with phone calls between sessions (if appropriate in your particular group) and to record and evaluate their experiences in their journals.

   ☞ *Set aside time at the next session to hear reports.*

## Variation

■ Tell group members to list one of their lower level fears, imagine they are facing it, and create an absurd solution. Ask them the following question: How do they feel? What impact does the humorous solution have on their level of anxiety? Follow with a group discussion that focuses on participants' "what if" fears.

# The Rational You and the Frightened You

Participants enhance their rational response by role-playing their Rational and Frightened Selves.

## Goals

To enhance participants' ability to think rationally about themselves.

To change participants' response patterns.

## Group Size

6–12.

## Time

1 hour minimum.

## Materials

Easel and easel paper; markers.

## Participant Preparation

Pages 47–69 of *Overcoming Panic, Anxiety, & Phobias* will help participants prepare for this session and will reinforce what they learn during the session.

## Process

1. Lead a discussion of anxious responses and rational responses, noting important points on the easel paper and pausing for questions and discussion after each point.

   ▪ You are all complex people and have many sides to your personalities. The two parts of you that are most important during your recovery from anxiety are the Rational You and the Frightened You.

   ▪ The Rational You analyzes information and is able to make decisions based on actual evidence. The Rational You acts a bit like a computer, guiding you through life, recognizing safety and danger based on past experience or sources of information. During anxious moments, the Rational You evaluates evidence for and against catastrophe.

■ Cognitive therapy, which is based on helping you look at the interaction between your thoughts, your feelings, and your behavior, is designed to help you get in touch with the Rational You. You learn to observe thoughts that come from the Frightened You and to respond to those thoughts more rationally.

■ Each of us also has a frightened side. When you develop excess anxiety or panic, the Frightened You takes over, pushing the Rational You to the side.

■ To overcome your anxiety, you must let the Rational You regain control. This is not easy. When you feel that you are in danger, you automatically want to protect yourself, and the Frightened You appears to provide protection.

■ As you continue to strengthen the Rational You, however, you will become more effective at evaluating your anxious beliefs.

■ As you begin to try some behavioral experiments using cognitive and exposure processes to help you approach that which you want to avoid, you will begin to get proof that you are actually safe even when you feel afraid.

■ Today, you will develop a dialogue between the Rational You and the Frightened You. During this dialogue, you will look at the messages that you are sending yourself.

■ The difference between having mild anxiety before giving a speech and fearing that you are going to make a complete fool of yourself may have something to do with the catastrophic messages that you are giving yourself.

■ If you are predicting the worst, total embarrassment, the Frightened You will take over, and your anxious feelings will intensify, keeping you in the anxiety cycle. The Frightened

You will give you increasingly scary messages. You will respond by becoming vigilant, monitoring all your body sensations and responding with even more anxiety.

■ If you can break into the anxiety cycle by having a dialogue with yourself during these scary situations, you will put the Rational You back in control.

2. Form two groups, A and B, and present the following instructions for the dialogue:

➤ Group A will play the Frightened You and Group B, the Rational You.

➤ One member of Group A will call out an anxious message.

➤ One or more members of Group B will then give the response of the Rational You.

➤ After everyone in Group A has offered an anxious message, the two groups will switch roles.

☞ *Be prepared to suggest a few anxious messages if members of Group A have difficulty generating ideas.*

3. When ideas begin to run out, lead a discussion of the process, encouraging participants to engage in an internal dialogue similar to this one.

## Variation

■ Allow participants to work in teams of two, each interviewing the other and presenting the other's rational as well as anxious thoughts to the group.

# Facing What I Fear in My Imagination

This exercise allows participants to face their fears in their own minds before they contemplate doing it in reality. The session should be led by a mental health professional.

### Goals

To prepare participants to face what they fear.

To reinforce participants sense that it is possible to think through anxiety or panic, that their minds can be more powerful than their fears.

To encourage participants to expose themselves in imagination to all their layers of worry or fear, to focus on their dreaded thoughts and sensations, and then to use their coping strategies.

### Group Size

6–10.

### Time

1–2 hour minimum.

### Materials

Pencils; **Facing What I Fear** worksheet.

### Participant Preparation

Pages 84–91 of *Overcoming Panic, Anxiety, & Phobias* will help participants prepare for this session and will reinforce what they learn during the session.

### Process

1. Introduce the exercise by acknowledging the difficulty of facing what we fear with the following comments:

   ▪ When people are afraid of something, whether their fear is reasonable or unreasonable, asking them to face the feared event, situation, or feeling—cold turkey, without preparation—can feel so overwhelming and terrifying that they are unable to follow through.

■ The fear is real, whatever the provocation, and the typical response to fear is self-protection, not exposure. Exposure to the feared situation, however, is essential for the fear to lessen.

■ One way for you to begin exposing yourself with relative safety to things that you fear is to conduct this exposure in your imagination. This process is effective preparation for confronting your fears in real life.

2. Distribute the **Facing What I Fear** worksheet and provide the following instructions, giving time for participants to complete each step:

➤ On the worksheet, list the situations, sensations, and thoughts you either try to avoid or can't get out of your mind.

➤ Rate each on a scale from 1 to 10 according to the intensity of your feelings.

3. Prepare participants to begin confronting one of their anxiety-provoking situations in their imagination, giving all of the following instructions before they begin.

➤ First, select one of the items with a rating of 5 or less.

➤ Then, close your eyes and begin to imagine yourself back in the anxiety-producing situation. Review the parts of the experience that make you most anxious, recalling your physical sensations and your thoughts or images, making the scene as vivid as possible. As with all exposure methods, you want to start with a milder fear and eventually work through the more feared items on your exposure list.

➤ As you notice your anxiety begin to rise, ignore the impulse to escape. Instead, make the most anxiety-provoking part of the scene even more vivid. You might want to overbreathe, tense your muscles, or perform whatever will bring on your usual anxiety symptoms. Keep focused on the most frightening part of your anxiety scenario, really being in it and living it.

➤ Try not to avoid your anxiety or distract yourself. If you begin to hold back, resist and allow yourself to feel the discomfort and stay with your scary thoughts. You want to bring on your anxiety instead of trying to reduce it during this part of the exercise. I will allow 10 minutes for this process.

4. After 10 minutes, continue with the following instructions:

➤ Now take a slow, gentle breath and picture the Rational You reassuring the Frightened You as you remain in the situation. Keep the scene in your mind and continue to practice your coping skills for the next 20 minutes.

➤ As you notice your fears diminish, experience and enjoy a feeling of success. Write down any new insights or self-talk you have gained as a result of this exercise.

5. Continue by asking participants to comment on their experience and leading a discussion of their comments.

6. Conclude the session with the following comments:

▪ You may have felt uncomfortable during this experience but notice that you were able to cope.

▪ It's important for you to practice this process regularly until you become comfortable exposing yourself in your imagination to every item on your list.

▪ You have just faced some of your fears and have used coping skills to calm yourself and challenge your anxiety. Record these strategies on your First Alert cards.

## Variation

▪ Participants imagine themselves experiencing anxiety, then managing it in a way that gives them a sense of mastery. This technique can be used to practice for success before a real-life anxiety situation.

## FACING WHAT I FEAR

List situations, thoughts or images, and physical sensations you are anxious or worried about or which may cause panic, then write a number from 1 to 10 that represents the intensity of your feelings.

Situations, thoughts or images, and                          Anxiety or
physical sensations                                          panic rating

_____    _____

_____    _____

_____    _____

_____    _____

_____    _____

_____    _____

_____    _____

_____    _____

_____    _____

_____    _____

_____    _____

# Bringing on the Symptoms of Anxiety and Panic

Participants use a variety of sensory exercises designed to induce their symptoms of panic or extreme anxiety. The session should be led by a mental health professional.

## Goals

To learn to bring on sensations of anxiety and panic and reduce the fear generated by these sensations.

To end avoidance of these feared sensations.

## Group Size

4–12.

## Time

1–2 hours.

## Materials

Pencils; **Sensory Exercise** worksheet.

## Participant Preparation

Pages 91–94 of *Overcoming Panic, Anxiety, & Phobias* will help participants prepare for this session and will reinforce what they learn during the session.

☞ *Use this exercise only with participants who have clearance from their physician. Supervise the sensory exercises of only four participants at a time. While others are waiting, they can read and discuss pages 75–106 of Overcoming Panic, Anxiety, & Phobias.*

## Process

1. Introduce the exercise with the following comments. Be prepared to reassure participants who may become anxious.

- When you are anxious or panicked, you may not be aware that fear of your own body sensations is bringing on your anxiety.

- Once you become aware that uncomfortable body sensations are not predictors of disaster, a change in your heartbeat or breathing will no longer lead to or intensify a panic attack.

- Today, you will experience some of these sensations in this controlled and safe environment with the help of therapists and the support of others in the group.

- At first, the body sensations may cause you to feel anxious. However, with practice you will find that the sensations remain, but the fear diminishes.

2. Distribute the **Sensory Exercise** worksheet and present the following instructions:

  ➤ Review the list of exercises and add others that you think might trigger physical sensations similar to those that you fear.

  ➤ After you try each activity for the specified amount of time, under the supervision of one of the group leaders, rate on a scale from 1 to 10 the intensity of the sensation and the intensity of the anxiety that it provoked.

  ➤ Then describe how the sensation relates to what you feel during a panic attack.

  ➤ Use your coping strategies—rational self-talk and calm, gentle breathing—until your anxiety is reduced to a level of 2, then repeat the entire exercise.

3. After working with each group, reconvene the entire group and conclude with the following comments:

  - Your courage in exposing yourself to these physical sensations has helped you take another step on the road to recovery.

  - Using the guidelines that your therapist has given you, continue to practice these sensory exercises until the anxiety produced by each activity is at a level of 2 or less.

  - You will discover as you continue to practice that you can experience the sensations without experiencing the fear.

# SENSORY EXERCISE

Add to the list of exercises below any others that trigger physical sensations similar to those that you fear. On a scale from 1 to 10, rate each sensation's intensity, then the intensity of the anxiety it provokes. On the next line, describe how this sensation relates to what you feel during anxiety.

Intensity of
Sensation / Anxiety

1. Hyperventilate (30 sec.) _____ _____

_____

2. Spin in a chair (1 min.) _____ _____

_____

3. Hold your breath (30 sec.) _____ _____

_____

4. Shake your head from side to side (30 sec.) _____ _____

_____

5. Run in place (30 sec.) _____ _____

_____

6. Bend quickly, then straighten up (30 sec.) _____ _____

_____

7. Rapidly run up and down stairs (30 sec.) _____ _____

_____

8. Put head between legs, then raise it (30 sec.) _____ _____

_____

_____ _____

_____

_____ _____

_____

# Putting It into Practice

In this essential exercise, participants prepare to expose themselves to situations that they fear, planning to break the exposure process into small, less intimidating components.

## Goals

To plan action steps for the exposure process.

## Group Size

6–12.

## Time

1–2 hours.

## Materials

Pencils; 3″ x 5″ index cards; easel and easel paper; markers; **My Goals** worksheet (p. 38); **Facing What I Fear** worksheet (p. 92).

## Participant Preparation

Pages 94–100 of *Overcoming Panic, Anxiety, & Phobias* will help participants prepare for this session and will reinforce what they learn during the session.

☞ *Participants should bring to this session the My Goals and Facing What I Fear worksheets, which they worked on in previous sessions. If they do not have these worksheets available, extra preparation time will be needed during this session.*

## Process

1. Introduce the exercise with the following comments, reinforcing them with brief notes on the easel paper:

   ■ During our sessions together, you have developed a variety of coping strategies for reducing your anxiety and you have experimented with these strategies in your imagination.

■ Now it is time to begin testing the techniques you have learned in real life. This process, although initially it may seem scary, is essential for you to gain confidence in your ability to manage your anxiety.

■ By putting yourself in a situation you have avoided and allowing yourself to experience and tolerate the physical sensations of anxiety, you can learn to lower your fear.

■ Today, you'll plan this exposure process, and next week you'll begin to implement your plan, which will consist of several parts. You will:

1) Select the anxiety-producing situation you would like to challenge.

2) Prepare your cognitive strategies, readying yourself to look at the odds and the danger that relate to your peril prediction.

3) Decide on relaxation techniques for your attention.

4) Prepare your action plan.

■ The longest journey begins with a single step. You've already taken many steps on your journey toward recovery. Exposing yourself to your fears will not be a giant leap; it will be another series of small steps—steps that you are now ready to take.

2. Ask participants to review the **Facing What I Fear** worksheet which they completed during a previous session and to select a situation with a relatively low anxiety rating for this first attempt at real-life exposure.

3. Distribute several 3 " x 5 " index cards to each participant. Give the following instructions for preparing First Alert cards. Pause for questions, encourage discussion, and give people time to complete writing after each step.

☞ *Prepare sample First Alert cards on easel paper. Using an example that is appropriate for your group, develop First Alert cards on the easel paper as you give instructions for participants to write on their own cards.*

➤ Today, you will prepare several First Alert cards, which you will carry with you when you enter the situation that you selected for your first experiment with real-life exposure. Write the following titles on four cards: Positive Self-Talk, Relaxation Techniques, Action Plan, and In Case of Difficulties.

➤ On the Positive Self-Talk card, write several statements from the Rational You about the odds of your peril prediction occurring and about the seriousness of the consequences if it does occur.

➤ On the Relaxation Techniques card, record one or more of the techniques that you found helped you release your tension: calm breathing, progressive muscle relaxation, a restful image, a calming cue word, or a mini-meditation.

➤ On the Action Plan card, record the specific steps you will take. For example, if you have difficulty entering a shopping mall:

✔ What day and time next week will you drive to the mall?

✔ Will you enter the mall and walk around, stand on the sidewalk outside, or just observe it from your car? Make that choice depending on your current level of anxiety.

✔ How long will you stay? It's important that you remain long enough for your anxiety to rise and then diminish. That's how you will prove to yourself that your uncomfortable body sensations are not dangerous.

✔ If you experience difficulties, how will you handle them?

✔ And finally, no matter what level of success you had, how will you congratulate and reward yourself for the great courage you showed in facing what you fear?

4. If time permits, participants can write action plan steps for other anxiety producing situations on their **My Goals** worksheet.

5. Conclude the session by encouraging participants to implement their plan prior to the next session and to be ready to share their experiences with other members of the group, knowing that everyone will support and applaud their efforts.

# Preparing Your Recovery Kit

This exercise is effective at one of the group's final sessions. Participants recall the ideas and techniques they've found most helpful and record on First Alert cards those they want to keep with them. The session should be led by a mental health professional.

## Goals

To review the principles and techniques learned in the group.

To put together the resources that will be most helpful to each person.

To illustrate the fact that different people prefer different coping techniques.

To reinforce the notion that setbacks are natural and that one should be prepared for them.

## Group Size

Unlimited.

## Time

20 minutes.

## Materials

Pencils; twenty 3" x 5"index cards for each participant; easel and easel paper; markers.

## Participant Preparation

Pages 107–116 of *Overcoming Panic, Anxiety, & Phobias* will help participants prepare for this session and will reinforce what they learn during the session.

## Process

1. Distribute twenty 3" x 5"index cards to each participant.

2. Ask participants to call out all the ideas and techniques they have found most helpful to them, and record their ideas on the easel paper. Encourage them to be brief, positive, and specific. If necessary, stimulate the discussion with some examples, selecting a few from this list:

- Paying attention to my breathing can help me relax.

- Anxiety is uncomfortable, but it is not dangerous.

- Thinking about something does not make it happen.

- Facing my anxiety makes me stronger.

- What are the odds that my fear will come true?

- I'm strong enough to handle even the worst thing I fear.

- I will notice my feelings, but I won't judge them.

- What are my five senses experiencing RIGHT NOW? What do I see, hear, smell, feel, and taste?

- If my anxiety level rises, I will try to assess and manage any stress factors in my life instead of blaming myself.

- If I begin to avoid driving again, I'll immediately set up an exposure plan and continue it until I can drive anywhere.

3. When the flow of ideas slows, give participants time to record on individual 3"x 5"index cards (First Alert cards), the ideas they find most useful. Suggest that participants carry these with them and consult them when they are under stress.

4. Encourage participants to add to their recovery kit as they discover new, effective strategies for reducing their anxiety.

# The Setback Opportunity

Members are provided with a list of six myths and facts about setbacks. The session should be led by a mental health professional.

## Goals

To reinforce the idea that recovery has its ups and downs.

To acquaint participants with techniques for coping with setbacks.

## Group Size

Unlimited.

## Time

20 minutes.

## Materials

Easel and easel paper; markers; **Myths and Facts about Setbacks** handout.

## Participant Preparation

Pages 107–116 of *Overcoming Panic, Anxiety, & Phobias* will help participants prepare for this session and will reinforce what they learn during the session.

## Process

1. Introduce the topic of setbacks with the following comments:

   ▪ As much as we would like it, there is no such thing as challenge-free recovery from anxiety problems.

   ▪ You've already begun the recovery process by participating in this group.

   ▪ You have many reasons to be proud of yourself. You're learning to view yourself as a person who can cope, and you've learned some techniques for doing so.

©1996 Whole Person Press 210 W Michigan Duluth MN 55802     (800) 247-6789

■ But even so, you can expect to have setbacks on your road to recovery, particularly in times of stress. The important thing is to be prepared for them and to know how to handle them.

■ Many people who have learned to handle their panic and anxiety attacks believe they are home free. When another attack occurs, they get discouraged and upset. This feeling of disappointment can make the panic, anxiety, or worry seem more out of control than it is. Even though you have made progress and are on the way to recovery, it seems you are back to square one. Your confidence is shaken; you become anxious about your anxiety, fearful about your fear.

2. Encourage participants to answer the following questions:

✔ Has anyone had an experience like this?

✔ How did it feel?

3. Continue your presentation about setbacks:

■ Although surprise and disappointment are natural reactions to a setback, setbacks are a normal part of the recovery process. In fact, if you think about it, they can only happen if progress has been made.

■ Setbacks are normal, predictable, and—most important— they can be managed. They provide opportunities to practice and consolidate what you know and to move ahead. When you can experience normal fluctuations in anxiety and worry without panicking and losing your connection to your newly improved self, you'll know that you're making progress toward recovery.

■ When you experience a setback, it is helpful to assess the conditions surrounding the setback and your reactions to it. This will help you get back on track during these frustrating but inevitable times.

■ Setbacks can happen for many reasons, and some of them are unavoidable. We make them more likely, however, by setting standards for ourselves that are too high or by being unforgiving of ourselves when we don't measure up.

©1996 Whole Person Press 210 W Michigan Duluth MN 55802      (800) 247-6789

■ Sometimes other feelings are mistaken for anxiety: sadness or anger, for instance. It's important to differentiate these feelings from fear.

■ Other factors that can contribute to stress and setbacks are the changes that occur naturally in our relationships precisely because we are recovering.

■ The setback cycle can become a closed circle in which stress and conflict lead to anxiety or panic symptoms, which in turn lead to catastrophic thinking, which leads to more severe anxiety or panic.

■ But while setbacks are inevitable, the setback cycle is not. You can avoid or break free of the cycle by remembering that you have the skills to choose another way. That way is the recovery cycle.

4. Distribute the **Myths and Facts about Setbacks** handout and instruct participants to take turns alternately reading the myths and the corresponding facts, prefacing each one with the word myth or the word fact.

5. Conclude by leading a discussion about setbacks and myths, encouraging participants to plan how they will let go of the myths that could trap them in the setback cycle.

# MYTHS AND FACTS ABOUT SETBACKS

| MYTHS | FACTS |
|---|---|
| 1. Setbacks are a sign of failure. | 1. Setbacks are not my fault. They are normal, to be expected, and a part of recovery. |
| 2. Setbacks mean I have to start all over. | 2. I have already learned many anxiety management strategies. It will take less time and effort to start using them again. I do not have to start all over again. |
| 3. Setbacks mean I'm never going to get better. | 3. Setbacks are signs of improvement. A setback can only come after an advance. That means I have made progress. |
| 4. Setbacks mean the worst panic or anxiety attack will come back and never leave. | 4. Setbacks are only temporary occurrences. I can gain increasing control over my anxiety. |
| 5. There is nothing good about a setback. | 5. Setbacks are opportunities to learn to manage anxiety in new ways. |
| 6. Setbacks mean I'm abnormal, that I'm hopeless. | 6. Setbacks are proof that I'm normal and that my progress to recovery is occurring. No one can master new skills without falling down and getting back up. |

©1996 Whole Person Press 210 W Michigan Duluth MN 55802     (800) 247-6789

# Breaking Free from the Setback Cycle

Participants analyze potential setbacks and plan coping strategies. The session should be led by a mental health professional.

## Goals

To make concrete and personalize the concepts of setbacks.

To begin anticipatory guidance in preparation for setbacks.

## Group Size

4–12.

## Time

30 minutes.

## Materials

Pencils; paper.

## Participant Preparation

Pages 107–116 of *Overcoming Panic, Anxiety, & Phobias* will help participants prepare for this session and will reinforce what they learn during the session.

## Process

1. Introduce the topic of setbacks with the following comments:

   ▓ If you've ever watched someone learn to ride a bike, you know that it's a process of small successes and a lot of wobbling and falling down. No one expects to do it perfectly the first time. In fact, falling down is an important part of learning how to ride.

   ▓ Learning to deal with anxiety reactions is a similar process— except that in addition to learning a new process, you also have old negative habits to unlearn.

■ Each failure can teach you something about what to do differently next time. Even when your anxiety is at its worst, the understanding and knowledge you have gained about yourself and about ways to break free will position you to move forward again.

2. Offer the following ten reminders and coping strategies for dealing with setbacks, encouraging participants to take notes:

   ■ Consult the notes that you've made on your First Alert cards; that's what they're for.

   ■ If you start to avoid out of fear, set up an exposure plan.

   ■ Challenge your anxious thoughts, and choose your response.

   ■ Remind yourself of the relaxation techniques you've learned, and use them.

   ■ Remember that setbacks are to be expected. They are a normal part of the recovery process.

   ■ Talk to yourself as though you were your best friend. Give yourself the calm support you deserve.

   ■ Review the records of your progress, and remind yourself that there are no setbacks without progress and no progress without setbacks.

   ■ Get support from friends and family, and possibly from a therapist.

   ■ Remember that setbacks are temporary and can be overcome.

   ■ In the meantime, stay active; don't let a setback disrupt your progress.

3. If the group has more than six participants, form smaller groups of four to six people. Give members of the small groups 15 minutes to talk with each other about the kinds of situations they think may trigger setbacks for them and to plan specific strategies they'll use when these setbacks occur.

4. Reconvene the entire group and give participants a chance to share each small group's insights.

# Recovery Enhancer
# Exercises

# Choosing Buddies

Participants team up with buddies with whom they will interact periodically during group sessions. They are encouraged to provide support for each other between sessions if they wish.

## Goal

To extend learning and provide mutual support between sessions.

## Group Size

Unlimited.

## Time

15 minutes.

## Materials

Pencils; paper.

## Process

☞ *To maximize the benefits of a buddy system, participants should be paired during the first or second session.*

1. Select a process for pairing participants. Possibilities include:
   - Participants choose their own buddies.
   - The leader assigns buddies based on the nature of participants' anxiety disorders.
   - Participants find buddies through a random selection process such as drawing names.

2. Explain to participants that having a buddy will give them a source of support between sessions if they wish.

3. Develop pairs using one of the processes described in step 1.

4. Encourage participants to exchange phone numbers and to make a plan for contacting each other between sessions.

# Fishing

After successfully confronting their anxiety, participants write short notes describing their accomplishments, then place the notes in a glass bowl.

## Goals

To provide encouragement and recognition to participants who successfully manage episodes of anxiety and panic.

To allow participants to learn from each other's successes.

## Group Size

Unlimited.

## Time

10 minutes for an explanation of the process, then a few minutes at each session.

## Materials

A glass bowl; pencils; small notepads.

## Process

1. Introduce the goals of this exercise by reminding participants that it takes great courage for them to expose themselves to situations that they fear and that this courage needs to be commended and celebrated.

2. Distribute small pieces of notepaper and pencils and provide the following instructions:

   ➤ When you have successfully practiced one of the coping techniques you are learning, on the notepaper I have provided, jot a sentence or two about your accomplishment.

   ➤ You may sign the note or write it anonymously.

➤ Fold the paper in half and place it in the glass bowl on the table. As the bowl fills, we'll see concrete evidence of the progress being made by each of you.

➤ At each session, I will fish out a few notes and read them. Then I'd like members of the group to show their support for the writer and the success story they shared on the note.

➤ Take a minute right now; think about the events of this past week and jot down your best attempt at coping with anxiety. Be sure to write the positive experiences rather than the negative ones. For example, looking at the grocery store or airport rather than avoiding the site as usual makes the next step toward recovery more attainable.

3. Collect the notes from the participants. At the end of the session, read one or two of them and encourage the group to cheer for the writer.

4. Fold the notes that have been read into quarters (to distinguish them from the unread ones) and put them back in the bowl.

©1996 Whole Person Press 210 W Michigan Duluth MN 55802     (800) 247-6789

# My First Anxiety Attack

If participants are prepared to address their problems publicly and verbally, this exercise will help them understand that others share their experiences and concerns.

## Goals

To allow participants to become used to hearing their concerns voiced aloud.

To reinforce the sense that, however strange they may think their particular anxiety problems are, others understand and have experienced similar problems and distress.

## Group Size

Unlimited.

## Time

1 hour.

## Materials

Easel and easel paper; markers; overhead.

## Participant Preparation

Pages 1–14 of *Overcoming Panic, Anxiety, & Phobias* will help participants prepare for this session and will reinforce what they learn during the session.

## Process

1. Introduce the exercise with the following comments, which are designed to help participants feel comfortable sharing their stories:

   ▪ Typically, when an anxiety problem develops, certain cues become associated with the onset of symptoms.

- The cues may be specific situations, thoughts, images, sensations, or life transitions.

- Anxiety responses can become so automatic and panic attacks so frightening that it is hard to focus on these early anxiety cues. As you become more aware of these cues, you can stop and analyze the situation before your anxiety escalates.

2. Give the following instructions:

➤ Today, I'd like each of you to take a few minutes and recall your very first attack of severe anxiety or panic. Many people find that even months or years later the details of that first attack are very clear. Try to remember them. (Pause for 2 minutes.)

➤ Now, if you are willing, I'd like you to share with the group an account of your first anxiety attack. This may feel uncomfortable to you, but it will help other people in our group.

➤ As you tell your story, I'm going to record the cues that you mention on the easel paper. Who will begin?

3. As participants tell their stories, record their anxiety cues on the easel paper in columns headed situations, thoughts, physical sensations, and behaviors.

4. After several people have shared their stories, use some of the following questions to stimulate discussion:

✔ We have heard about lots of uncomfortable situations, scary thoughts, and unpleasant physical symptoms. How are these impacting your life now?

✔ Have your symptoms become worse or better since they first began?

✔ What have you tried to do to decrease or eliminate your anxiety symptoms?

5. Make the following points to help participants understand why their first anxiety attack had such a powerful and long-lasting effect on them.

■ Memories of your first anxiety attack can be very powerful.

■ We all remember traumatic events more clearly and intensely than the mundane happenings of daily life. We remember these events because of the strong emotional impact that is caused by extreme excitement.

■ In the case of anxiety attacks, the sensations can be so severe that we begin to scan our bodies for any sign that we may be in danger again. If we are used to worrying a lot, we can begin to live our lives in such a way as to always be on guard for the worst to happen.

■ During your recovery program you will learn specific strategies to overcome your anxiety.

6. Conclude the session by presenting the following information as you encourage participants' hopes for recovery.

■ By now, you may have tried all kinds of ways to contain your anxiety. Sometimes you may be successful, and sometimes it just seems to get worse. Your anxiety may have spread to many other situations since your initial attack or become more intolerable in its original form.

■ The anxiety may flood over you, unexplained and unstoppable. More than anything else, you probably want to put it out of your mind and never have to think about it.

■ Rather than ignoring your symptoms, however, I'm going to encourage you to analyze them as a first step toward controlling them.

■ You may be participating in this group hoping a miracle will happen, but feeling pretty hopeless that things will ever get better. After all, your experiences so far may have been very disappointing even with all your efforts.

■ By coming to the group, you have made an important step toward mastering your anxiety or panic. As you continue to participate in this program, your anxiety problems can become dim memories, and you can lose the overwhelming fear that is stealing your freedom to enjoy life.

## Variations

- Ask participants to form pairs and interview each other, then allow them to tell each other's story.

- If the group is large, form groups of three or four participants, then allow each group to describe its problems as a unit.

# Thought Map

This paper and pencil exercise gives participants new insights about their anxiety.

## Goals

To strengthen participants' ability to describe their anxiety.

To promote understanding of the interrelationships between various facets of their anxiety problem.

To stimulate new insights about their problem.

## Group Size

Unlimited.

## Time

1 hour.

## Materials

Pencils; paper; easel and easel paper; markers.

## Participant Preparation

Pages 1–6 of *Overcoming Panic, Anxiety, & Phobias* will help participants prepare for this session and will reinforce what they learn during the session.

## Process

1. Introduce the goals of this exercise with the following comments:

   ▪ Often we become locked into a single way of looking at a problem.

   ▪ Finding new ways to think about it can give us fresh insights and suggest new ways of coping.

   ▪ Today, I'll ask you to try an activity called idea mapping or networking.

2. Demonstrate idea mapping on the easel paper by writing a single word, such as picnic, in the middle of the page and giving the following instructions:

   ➤ Begin calling out words that are related to the word in the middle of this page. I'll write your words on the paper around my word.

   ➤ As the new words are added, feel free to call out words that relate to them, not just to the original word.

3. Write the words that are called out, clustering them as seems appropriate. When ideas stop flowing freely, draw a circle around each word, then give the following instructions:

   ➤ Lots of words and ideas are now on this paper. Some of them are clearly related to each other. Some seem unrelated. In other cases, the relationships are subtle rather than obvious. Begin thinking about the possible connections between these words.

   ➤ Call out the relationships that come to your mind. I'll begin: Ants eat the picnic food.

4. Continue to draw lines and to help people see relationships. The example below suggests how the paper might look when the example is complete.

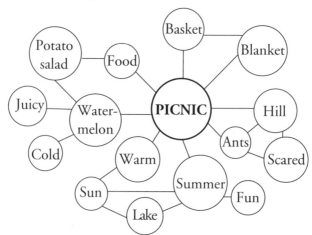

5. Distribute paper and pencils and give the following instructions:

   ➤ You will now have the opportunity to use idea mapping to gain new insights about your anxiety.

   ➤ Begin by writing all the words that pop into your mind in response to the phrase "the life story of my anxiety."

   ➤ If a word occurs to you, write it down. Don't judge it and eliminate it.

   ➤ When one word that you write makes you think of other words, place them in a cluster.

   ➤ When your paper is filled with words, draw circles around them, then begin drawing lines between the circles as connections occur to you.

6. Give participants 15 minutes to complete this process, then conclude the session by asking participants to share their insights about one cluster of words from their paper.

## Variations

▪ Select another theme for the writing assignment such as "how I feel when I'm anxious."

▪ Following the writing period, divide the group into pairs to discuss their word maps and what they learned from the exercise.

# Word Toss

Participants list the thoughts and physical sensations that describe their anxiety. Each individual then shares some of these words and phrases as a group list is compiled.

## Goals

To help members think explicitly and analytically about anxiety problems and to approach assessment through their own experience.

To prepare for a more structured assessment.

## Group Size

Unlimited.

## Time

20 minutes.

## Materials

Pencils; paper; easel and easel paper; markers.

## Participant Preparation

Pages 1–6 of *Overcoming Panic, Anxiety, & Phobias* will help participants prepare for this session and will reinforce what they learn during the session.

## Process

1. Distribute pencils and paper to participants, then introduce this word toss exercise with the following comments:

   ■ We often get new insights when we toss ideas out rapidly without analyzing or prejudging them.

   ■ I'm going to give you 5 minutes to write down all the words and phrases that come to your mind when you think about your anxiety.

- Perhaps the ideas that come to your mind will concern physical sensations such as a rapid heartbeat or nausea. Or perhaps you will first think of images such as falling off a cliff or emotions such as the fear of dying.

- Don't stop to analyze your words and phrases, just write them down as quickly as you can.

2. After 5 minutes, invite participants to mention some of the words and phrases that are most meaningful for them and write them on the easel paper.

3. Conclude by pointing out that participants are not alone in their journey toward recovery. Others have the same uncomfortable and frightening symptoms that trouble them.

**Variation**

- Instead of asking individuals to write words and phrases, the group can brainstorm them as the leader writes them on easel paper.

©1996 Whole Person Press 210 W Michigan Duluth MN 55802    (800) 247-6789

# My Recovery Story

A first-person story of anxiety recovery is distributed to the group. They are asked to write their own story during the session and at home in the following week. (Each week thereafter, one or two recovery stories can be shared with the group.) The session should be led by a mental health professional.

## Goals

To stimulate participants' imaginations about their own recovery.

To encourage the use of writing as a means of expression and healing.

To support participants as they consider strategies that could be helpful in their own recovery.

## Group Size

Unlimited.

## Time

1 hour.

## Materials

A copy of one of the recovery stories printed in *Overcoming Panic, Anxiety, & Phobias* or another inspiring recovery story; pencils; paper.

## Process

1. Introduce the session by telling the group that you (or one of the participants) will read a true story about how one person recovered from severe anxiety.

2. Read the story expressively.

3. Lead a discussion of people's feelings about the story by making the following comments:

- When people read recovery stories, they usually are pleased to know that others share similar problems and that it is possible to recover.

- Many people, however, have doubts that they, too, can get better.

4. Ask participants whether the story makes them feel hopeful or discouraged about their own prospects for recovery.

5. Encourage participants to imagine what life will be like when they recover from their anxiety. Distribute pencils and paper and give the following instructions:

   ➤ Imagine your own recovery story; think about the process, all the things you will be able to do easily and comfortably, and the feelings that you will have about life and about yourself.

   ➤ Now take a few minutes to write your story, making it as real as possible.

6. After 10 minutes, ask participants if anyone would like to read their story to the group.

7. Conclude the exercise by explaining to participants that imagining their recovery story is a powerful way of reinforcing their journey toward recovery. Encourage them to record in their journals where they hope to be in one month, six months, one year, and five years and to discuss their hopes and dreams with other participants.

## Variation

- Participants could write their stories at home rather than during the group session.

# The Mind-Body Connection in Action

To demonstrate the mind's effect on the body, participants notice how their body is affected by the mere sight of a familiar food.

**Goal**

To demonstrate the mind-body connection.

**Group Size**

Unlimited.

**Time**

5–10 minutes, depending on the size of the group.

**Materials**

One lemon.

**Participant Preparation**

Pages 35–41 of *Overcoming Panic, Anxiety, & Phobias* will help participants prepare for this session and will reinforce what they learn during the session.

**Process**

1. Introduce the mind-body connection by observing that our minds can have a powerful effect on our bodies. Tell participants that they will have a chance to observe this for themselves.

2. Tell participants to pass from person to person the lemon that you have provided.

3. Ask participants how their bodies responded to the sight of and to thinking about the lemon.

4. Encourage participants to recognize that many physical symptoms of anxiety are brought on by their minds. This is natural,

but as they become aware of the effect their minds have on their bodies, they will be able to use coping strategies to manage their physical symptoms.

5. Conclude the exercise by suggesting that participants be alert to the mind-body connection and that they record their observations in their journals.

# Mindful Eating

Participants experience mindfulness by slowly and thoughtfully eating a few raisins.

## Goals

To experience mindfulness, an attitude that is at the heart of meditation.

To acquire a technique that can be used at any time and in any place to calm the mind and body.

## Group Size

Unlimited.

## Time

10 minutes.

## Materials

Three raisins per person.

☞ *Some participants may not like raisins, so it would be sensible to provide another bite-size food.*

## Participant Preparation

Pages 35–41 of *Overcoming Panic, Anxiety, & Phobias* will help participants prepare for this session and will reinforce what they learn during the session.

## Process

☞ *This exercise can be carried out in a lighthearted way. To achieve the desired attentiveness, however, it should be done in silence except for the facilitator's commentary.*

1. Introduce the activity with the following comments:

- Mindfulness, or nonjudging attentiveness, can be applied in every sphere of life.

- If you practice focusing your attention on being fully in the moment while engaged in an activity, you will find that this process can become a coping strategy for dealing with anxiety.

- Today you will have an opportunity to experience mindfulness in respect to eating, an activity we often do with very little awareness.

- Most of us have eaten many raisins in our lifetimes, but we may never have paid specific attention to the process of eating the raisin and observing ourselves moment to moment.

2. Distribute three raisins to each person and begin the activity by giving the following instructions:

   ➤ Observe the look and feel of your raisins, noticing their textures, colors, and shapes.

   ➤ Close your eyes and hold the raisins close to your nose so you can focus on their smell.

3. Invite participants to begin eating their raisins very slowly as they follow your instructions, which you should present one step at a time.

   ➤ Place one raisin in your mouth.

   ➤ Slowly begin to chew the raisin, paying attention to its taste, how it feels on your tongue, how your mouth and throat work as you swallow.

   ➤ See if you can focus your entire attention on the act of eating the raisin. Let any thoughts that arise in your mind float away without following them.

   ➤ When you finish the first raisin, enjoy the lingering taste and take your time before putting the second one in your mouth.

   ➤ Eat the second raisin as slowly and mindfully as you can.

   ➤ Continue until you have eaten all three raisins. If you find your mind straying, simply bring it back to your current activity of eating.

©1996 Whole Person Press 210 W Michigan Duluth MN 55802     (800) 247-6789

➤ Use your breathing to help you stay focused. I will be silent now so we can concentrate on our mindful eating.

4. Allow 4–5 minutes for participants to eat their raisins. Join them in this activity.

5. Lead a discussion of the experience using some of the following questions:

✔ What was this experience like for you?

✔ Did you become impatient? critical? restless?

✔ What thoughts went through your mind?

✔ Did you find it easy or difficult to set distracting thoughts aside and focus on this single activity?

6. Encourage participants to try this exercise at home with raisins, grapes, or other bite-size food and then with an entire meal. Suggest that they try to give this kind of mindful attentiveness to an activity such as taking a walk or doing a task. They should record their experiences in their journals.

©1996 Whole Person Press 210 W Michigan Duluth MN 55802      (800) 247-6789

# Train of Thought

Participants learn to observe their thoughts without pursuing them. The image of a train of thought is used, and participants are given time to focus on this image.

## Goals

To explain the concept of detachment from one's thoughts.

To offer experience in observing but not pursuing thoughts.

## Group Size

Unlimited.

## Time

10 minutes.

## Materials

None.

## Participant Preparation

Pages 5, 6, 35–41 of *Overcoming Panic, Anxiety, & Phobias* will help participants prepare for this session and will reinforce what they learn during the session.

## Process

1. Introduce the goals of the session by making the following comments:

   ■ Observing thoughts but not following them is an important part of relaxing and achieving freedom from stress and tension. This kind of detachment is key to remaining in the present rather than worrying about the past or future.

   ■ An image that may be helpful is based on the familiar expression "train of thought." We wouldn't dream of getting on board a train every time we saw one, even if it came to a complete stop, and we were personally invited to do so! We wouldn't think of leaving our present lives and obligations so impulsively. Yet we spend much of our lives hopping onto the trains of thought that pass through our heads, leaving behind whatever we were doing when they come chugging by.

■ When those thought-trains are filled with fears and what-if's, this habit of being carried away by our thoughts can be quite damaging. It's especially important, then, that we stand our ground and resist the temptation and the habit of getting on board.

2. Invite participants to close their eyes and imagine the following scene as you read it very slowly:

*Imagine yourself doing something you enjoy and care about—maybe gardening, reading a book, or talking with a loved one. (30 second pause) You hear a train whistle in the distance, headed your way. Soon it is close enough for you to see it and to feel the way it resonates in the ground.*

*The train is slowing down now. It's going slower and slower. . . slow enough that you could hop aboard just like the hobos in old movies . . . but you don't do so. Instead, you stay put, right where you are. As the train slowly chugs past you and begins to pick up speed, you observe its color . . . its contents . . . the signs painted on it. Maybe you guess where it's been and think about where it may be heading . . . but you stay where you are.*

*After observing the train briefly, you resume your former activity and don't give the train another thought. It was of passing interest, and now it's gone.*

3. Lead a discussion of this process by asking participants to comment on the following points:

■ You can cultivate this same observant attitude toward your thoughts—noting your thoughts without reacting to them.

©1996 Whole Person Press 210 W Michigan Duluth MN 55802      (800) 247-6789

- It's important to practice this process during times when you are least anxious.

- As you become more and more proficient at observing your thoughts, you can use this coping strategy to manage anxiety.

- When you do this, do not reject your anxious thoughts or try to ignore them. Just allow them to occur while you remain detached. It might be helpful to imagine them passing by on a train, eventually traveling out of your consciousness.

- This imagery exercise is followed by a group discussion of the observations and insights members gained as a result of it. (Allow 10–15 minutes for this discussion.)

4. Encourage participants to practice this process during the week and to make notes in their journals.

# Using an Image to Relax

Participants experience guided imagery and learn how this process can help them relax.

## Goals

To achieve a state of relaxation.

To familiarize participants with the experience of using an image to relax, making it easier for them to do so on their own.

## Group Size

Unlimited.

## Time

20 minutes.

## Materials

None.

## Participant Preparation

Pages 37–40 of *Overcoming Panic, Anxiety, & Phobias* will help participants prepare for this session and will reinforce what they learn during the session.

## Process

1. Briefly introduce the concept and benefits of guided imagery.

2. Ask participants to make themselves comfortable and to sit quietly for a moment.

3. Invite participants to close their eyes, as you slowly and softly read the following narration:

> *You are going to spend some time now in a place where you feel safe and full of a sense of well-being. It is beside a pool of quiet water that reflects the rays of the sun on a gently*

*warm day. You are seated comfortably at the edge of the pool,
soaking up the sun's warmth and looking at the reflections in
the water. As you begin to see the pool in your mind's eye,
place it in an outdoor setting where you feel especially
comfortable. That may be in a mountain meadow . . . in the
city park . . . in your backyard . . . in a favorite place you
recall from your childhood. (20 second pause)*

*Take a few moments now, and fill in the details in your
mind's eye, as you would if you were drawing this picture.
Surround your pool with your favorite plants and flowers.
Place a few small objects around that make this spot special
for you—smooth pebbles, flowers, flavorful herbs, bits of wood
or leaves. Notice the warmth of the sun . . . the soft murmur
of the breeze ruffling the water . . . the scent of the
flowers . . . the chirping of birds or the melodious sound of
wind chimes, or perhaps the laughter of children far in the
distance. Sit quietly in this peaceful place and soak it in. Use
your slow, gentle breathing to deepen your presence there.
(2–3 minute pause)*

*You can come back to this place whenever you need to be
refreshed and feel its safety and comfort. Now it is time to
leave, though, to go back to a place where you may be less
comfortable.*

*Imagine yourself now moving from your place of safety
into a place that causes you some anxiety, but hold on to the
feeling you had while sitting next to your pool (30 second
pause). The feelings of calmness and safety you had beside
your pool are available to you whenever you choose to tune
into them. Just allow yourself to experience the same sensations of comfort and calm in this more stressful place. Remember that your slow, gentle breathing can also help you.
(3 minute pause)*

*Before we bring our attention out of the places we have
been and come back together as a group, take a moment to*

*revisit your peaceful pool. Take a mental snapshot of it. The
mental snapshot will be there for you when you want to
return to that place. Now, gently turn your attention back to
the sound of my voice, the presence of the other members of
the group, the chair you're sitting on, the room we are in
together. When you're ready, open your eyes. Take a nice deep
breath while I count—inhale, 2, 3, 4, 5, 6, hold, 2, 3, exhale,
2, 3, 4, 5, 6. Good. (Brief pause)*

4. Invite the group to discuss their experience by asking some of the
   following questions:

   ✔ Did you find it easy or difficult to visualize yourself beside the
     pool?

   ✔ What changes in your body did you notice during the time
     that you imagined yourself by the pool?

   ✔ Were there changes in your body sensations when you
     imagined the more stressful situation?

   ✔ How did it work when you tried to recall your feelings of calm
     by the pool?

5. Conclude the exercise by encouraging participants to write in their
   journals about their experiences and to set aside some time in the
   next day or two to try to revisit their peaceful imaginary pools.

## Variations

- Group time can be taken for journal writing.

- Participants can get together with their buddies to compare
  experiences.

©1996 Whole Person Press 210 W Michigan Duluth MN 55802    (800) 247-6789

# Myths and Realities

People who suffer from severe anxiety can be trapped by the apparent hopelessness of their situation. This exercise can be a valuable way to introduce participants to the ways in which their own thoughts may be hindering their recovery. The session should be led by a mental health professional.

## Goals

To strengthen each participant's awareness of and authority over their own thinking.

To reinforce each participant's sense that it is possible to see through even the cognitive manifestations of anxiety or panic.

To support participants in gathering evidence for their beliefs and learning to evaluate their thoughts.

## Group Size

Unlimited as an introductory workshop or lecture, 6–10 if used with an ongoing group.

## Time

1 hour minimum.

## Materials

Pencils; paper; easel and easel paper; markers.

## Participant Preparation

Pages 47–66 of *Overcoming Panic, Anxiety, & Phobias* will help participants prepare for this session and will reinforce what they learn during the session.

## Process

1. Introduce the topic by making the following comments about the overwhelming effects of anxiety:

■ As many of you are aware, anxiety can affect your bodies, causing unpleasant, even frightening symptoms.

■ You are also aware of the effect of anxiety on your emotions: the fear, depression, and discouragement that often accompany it.

■ You may, however, be less aware of the way anxiety can affect your thoughts. Today, we're going to look at how even our thinking becomes confused by the irrational thoughts that accompany anxiety and panic attacks.

2. Distribute pencils and paper and give the following instructions:

➤ On this paper, list all the things that you believe to be true when you are anticipating or in the midst of an anxiety episode or a panic attack.

Your list may include thoughts such as:

■ I'm so inadequate that I'll probably be fired.

■ My hands are sweating so much, everyone I shake hands with will know how I feel.

■ My baby may die of crib death if I don't check on her every few minutes.

■ My heart is pounding so hard, I think I'm going to have a heart attack.

➤ Don't edit your ideas. Just write them as fast as you can, trying to remember every fearful belief that you have had.

3. When most people appear to be done writing, ask participants to call out the beliefs they listed as you record them on the easel paper. Select several of the most commonly offered beliefs and, working with them one at a time, ask participants to give all the evidence they have in support of that belief.

☞ *Use a new page of easel paper for each belief. Write the belief at the top of the paper, then head two columns "evidence for" and "evidence against." Record participants' comments in the appropriate column.*

4. When the "evidence for" list seems to be complete, ask participants to give all the evidence they can against the belief they are
   considering.

5. When both lists are complete, ask participants to review them
   and decide whether there really is any objective evidence that
   supports the belief.

6. If objective evidence does exist, ask participants to consider what
   kinds of beliefs might reasonably be based upon that evidence.

## Variations

- Allow participants to work in teams of two, each interviewing the
  other and presenting the other's beliefs and evidence to the group.

- Allow participants to work in teams of three or four, beginning
  with the proposition that none of the group members' beliefs are
  founded in fact. Then instruct each group to come up with a set
  of ten beliefs about the nature of each group member's anxiety
  problems, individually and severally, that they know to be true
  and can prove.

# Roadblocks to Change

People who suffer from anxiety may find that although they have made substantial progress on their way to recovery, roadblocks seem to keep them from reaching their goal.

## Goals

To identify, manage, and eliminate each participant's roadblocks to change.

To reinforce each participant's sense that it is possible to reduce anxiety, stress, or panic by thinking through their cognitive habits and by changing their own response patterns accordingly.

## Group Size

Unlimited.

## Time

1 hour minimum; additional sessions can be helpful.

## Materials

Pencils; paper; easel and easel paper; markers; **Roadblocks to Change** worksheet.

## Participant Preparation

Pages 15–27, 107–116 of *Overcoming Panic, Anxiety, & Phobias* will help participants prepare for this session and will reinforce what they learn during the session.

## Process

1. Introduce the concept of roadblocks by drawing a curving line on the easel paper and identifying it as a road. Ask the following questions to help participants understand that on an automobile journey, a variety of obstacles can make it difficult to reach a destination. As participants list obstacles, illustrate them with

©1996 Whole Person Press 210 W Michigan Duluth MN 55802      (800) 247-6789

simple symbols (for instance, a squashed circle for a flat tire) and distribute the symbols along the line.

✔ On a journey by car, what situations might develop that could make it difficult for you to reach your destination?

✔ If this was an important journey, would you let these road-blocks force you to stop or turn back?

✔ How could you conquer each of these roadblocks?

2. Help participants understand the application of the roadblock metaphor to anxiety issues by making the following comments:

▪ The longer and more significant the journey, the more likely it is that roadblocks will be encountered.

▪ Your journey toward recovery is one of the most important journeys that you will ever make.

▪ It is essential that you not let various roadblocks keep you from reaching your goal—freedom from excess worry and fear, freedom to do whatever you would like to do, and freedom to find pleasure in life.

▪ Since you have already made progress toward recovery, it is likely that you have already met some roadblocks. You may have conquered them, or they may still be holding you back.

3. Distribute the **Roadblocks to Change** worksheet and give the following instructions:

➤ On the worksheet, use a symbol or a few words to record the roadblocks you have met and the ones that you think you may face in the future. I will allow 5 minutes for you to do this.

➤ If you have conquered a roadblock, make a few notes on how you did it. Your experience will help others in the group.

➤ Ask participants to call out the roadblocks they recorded on their worksheet and list them on the easel paper. Leave plenty of space so that solutions can also be recorded.

4. Taking the roadblocks one at a time, ask participants to brain-storm how people can get past these obstacles. Allow those who

have conquered a particular roadblock to begin by offering their solutions.

5. Summarize the discussion by commenting that when a roadblock seems insurmountable, it is wise to stop and ask a few questions:

   ✔ How can I get back on track? Exactly what is the nature of this problem?

   ✔ Can I help myself remove the roadblock, or do I need help? If so, who could help?

6. Use the following remarks to conclude the session on an encouraging note.

   ▪ Read the recovery stories in *Overcoming Panic, Anxiety, & Phobias*. All of those people faced obstacles, but they overcame them. You can too!

   ▪ You probably look at obstacles to recovery as roadblocks. They can be very discouraging. However, they are really part of everyone's recovery.

   ▪ Recovery from a problem is usually an up and down process. Imagine yourself driving along a rolling or curvy highway. As you drive along, it's really hard to see the direction in which you're going or to know whether you're making progress.

   ▪ It's important to know your destination and to understand the nature of your journey, because if you take a short view it can be difficult to determine whether you're really getting anywhere. Taking a longer view and keeping your mind focused on your final goal will help you establish more realistic expectations of what's involved in your journey to recovery. You will be less likely to interpret trouble spots as insurmountable.

   ▪ You need to be prepared for roadblocks to change because if you are expecting a smooth journey and encounter difficulties, you'll find it easier to cope if you've thought of how to do it ahead of time. If you are not prepared for difficulties, the first trouble spot may cause you to give up the trip.

■ Exhaustion can be a major roadblock. Travel can be tiring. Anyone who has taken a long trip is aware of that. Your journey to recovery may be physically, mentally, and emotionally challenging and exhausting, and you may want to quit before you reach your destination. You're almost there, but not quite—and you're tired.

Perhaps you can drive on the freeway during mid-morning but not during rush hour. Or you may be able to conduct a departmental meeting without undue anxiety but not a managers' meeting.

■ It's essential that you continue on your journey. If you don't travel forward and complete your journey to recovery, the risk of slipping back is great.

■ You're not alone on your journey. This group will provide support; everyone here understands what you are facing, and you, of course, can help others in the group.

## Variations

■ Allow participants to work in teams of two, each interviewing the other about each other's roadblocks.

■ Devote additional sessions to removing successive roadblocks, until each participant's roadblocks have been eliminated.

## ROADBLOCKS TO CHANGE

**Recovery**

**Anxiety**

# Here Comes the Judge

A variation on role playing, this exercise both encourages each participant to see their situation from all sides, allowing their rational self greater scope. The session should be led by a mental health professional.

## Goals

To strengthen each participant's critical faculties in evaluating his or her problem.

To reinforce each participant's creative participation in finding solutions to his or her problem.

## Group Size

6-12.

## Time

1 hour minimum; may be repeated.

## Materials

Pencils; paper.

## Participant Preparation

Pages 47–66 of *Overcoming Panic, Anxiety, & Phobias* will help participants prepare for this session and will reinforce what they learn during the session.

## Process

1. Introduce the exercise by telling participants that this role-playing activity will help them respond more rationally when their anxiety begins to escalate.

2. Form groups of three people and give the following instructions:

➤ Your anxiety may be having a criminal effect on your life by stealing the joy from it, by destroying relationships, and by robbing you of hope. Let's put that anxiety on trial.

➤ First, we need a defendant, a defense attorney, and a prosecutor. Take 1 minute and decide which person in your group will take each role.

➤ Next you will work out your role play, scripting a scene in which the defendant's anxiety response is put on trial. Your script should be just a series of notes, reminders of points that each participant in the role play wants to make.

The scenario should proceed as follows:

▪ The defense attorney questions the defendant to elicit a description of the anxiety problem.

▪ The prosecution questions the defendant, challenging the truth of the evidence that has been presented.

▪ In rebuttal, the defense again questions the defendant, attempting to get more evidence for the defendant's anxiety.

▪ In counterrebuttal, the prosecution tries to shake the defendant's testimony, pointing out through questioning the ways in which it is not rational and concluding with a statement about the negative effect anxiety is having on the defendant's life.

3. After the scripts have been completed, reconvene the entire group and ask for volunteers to present their role play. Encourage the rest of the group, the jury, to ask additional questions. Conclude the role play by asking the jury to vote on the guilt or innocence, not of the defendant, but of the defendant's anxiety.

4. If time allows, ask each group to present its role play. Then have participants return to their small groups, rotate roles, and develop a new scenario.

# Attitude Traps

Participants often long for a dramatic breakthrough, some new revelation that will solve their problem forever. Such revelations are unlikely, of course, but their desire for them can be a powerful therapeutic tool in itself.

## Goals

To provide a new way for participants to imagine their own recovery.

To reinforce participants' creative participation in finding solutions to their anxiety problems.

## Group Size

Unlimited; 6–12 for group process.

## Time

1 hour minimum; may be repeated.

## Materials

Pencils; paper; easel and easel paper; markers.

## Participant Preparation

Pages 1–27 of *Overcoming Panic, Anxiety, & Phobias* will help participants prepare for this session and will reinforce what they learn during the session.

## Process

1. Introduce the exercise by asking participants to brainstorm words and images that are suggested by the word "trap." If they have difficulty, you may need to ask questions that will lead them to think of enclosures such as cages and locked rooms, physical restraints such as leg traps, handcuffs, chains, and visual

constraints such as stop signs. Write the words and images on the easel paper.

2. Tell participants to close their eyes and to imagine themselves caught in a trap from which they finally break free. To help make this imaginary scenario real, ask the following questions:

✔ What does the trap that you're caught in look like?

✔ What do you look like and how do you feel—lonely? frightened? angry?

✔ Imagine yourself breaking free. How could you do that?

✔ What would the consequences of freedom be?

3. Distribute pencils and paper and ask participants to write or draw the scenario that they just imagined.

4. Ask participants who are willing to share their pictures or stories with the group. If they do not draw the connection between the trap they have written about or drawn and their anxiety, call it to their attention. Encourage the entire group to focus their discussion on breaking free and its consequences.

**Variation**

■ Allow participants to work in teams, actually staging one or two stories written by its members, each member of the group taking one part.

# Introducing My Alter Ego

Participants introduce and briefly describe their nonanxious alter egos as though they were other people.

## Goals

To help members focus on aspects of their identities other than anxiety.

To help members, by implication, set goals for recovery.

To help members see these dimensions in each other, relate to each other's strengths, and be supportive of this stronger identity.

## Group Size

Unlimited, as long as enough time is allowed—group can be divided in smaller groups of 4–6.

## Time

2–5 minutes per person; 20 minutes to 3 hours depending on size of group.

## Materials

Pencils; paper.

## Participant Preparation

Page 48 of *Overcoming Panic, Anxiety, & Phobias* will help participants prepare for this session and will reinforce what they learn during the session.

## Process

1. Introduce the concept of an alter ego, making the following comments:

   ■ Often people appear quite different with different groups. They may be lighthearted and playful with children, focused and intent with coworkers, anxious with their boss, and relaxed with only a few friends.

- It sometimes takes a few moments to recognize a person in an environment other than the usual. It may appear that we are seeing an alter ego, a second or different personality.

- Since you are participating in a group that is focusing on panic and other anxiety disorders, you have probably been displaying only one side of your personality, that of an anxious person. But you do have a nonanxious alter ego.

- If your anxiety has been overwhelming, that nonanxious alter ego may be pretty well hidden. You may have to remember it or imagine it, but that's what I'd like you to do today.

2. Give the following instructions:

   ➤ Think for a few minutes about your nonanxious alter ego, the person you can imagine yourself being when you recover from anxiety. In a few minutes, I'm going to ask you to introduce that person to the group. Let me give you an example by telling you about my alter ego (Modify the following example in a way that is appropriate for you.):

   *I'd like you to meet Alexandra. She has been a singer since she was a child, and she loves performing and being in the spotlight. She says she feels nervous before she goes on stage, but knows how to use the tension to her advantage and never feels uneasy once she starts to sing. Her favorite activity is singing flamboyant solos in front of a huge, adoring crowd.*

   ➤ Use the next ten minutes to imagine and make a few notes on your nonanxious alter ego. Let your imagination run wild.

3. Ask members to give their alter ego a name and to introduce it to the group.

4. Conclude the exercise by encouraging participants to keep imagining their alter ego and the fun they will have with that aspect of their personality when it is free to express itself.

## Variations

- After participants describe their alter ego, others in the group can suggest names that seem appropriate for the alter ego's personality.

- Give participants colored pens or crayons and paper on which to draw a picture of their nonanxious alter ego—perhaps a series of drawings of their alter ego engaged in a variety of activities, activities their anxious self would be hesitant to engage in even though they would love to do so.

# I Should

This exercise provides a simple way to encourage participants to look at their thought patterns, think them through, and come up with strategies to alter their unrealistic expectations of themselves.

## Goals

To provide participants with a simple, straightforward way of identifying, analyzing, and treating their own perfectionist thoughts.

To reinforce each participant's sense that it is possible for them to think about anxiety in new ways.

## Group Size

6–12.

## Time

1–2 hours.

## Materials

Pencils; paper.

## Participant Preparation

Pages 66–69 of *Overcoming Panic, Anxiety, & Phobias* will help participants prepare for this session and will reinforce what they learn during the session.

## Process

1. Introduce the exercise by making the following points about perfectionism:

   ▪ People with anxiety problems often have problems with perfectionism—holding themselves to impossibly high standards.

   ▪ You may be a perfectionist without realizing it. You may have thought of yourself as a failure for so long that you don't recognize that no one could meet the standards you have set for yourself.

- Most of us recognize that it is not wise to pressure children by expecting them to perform above their abilities. They will become anxious and discouraged if they rarely or never succeed.

- By setting impossibly high standards for yourself, you can guarantee yourself a similar outcome—anxiety and depression.

2. Distribute paper and pencils and give the following directions:

➤ With vertical lines, divide your paper into three columns.

➤ Write the words "I should" at the top of the first column, "Advantages" at the top of the second column, and "Disadvantages" at the top of the third column.

➤ In the first column, list as many phrases as possible that complete the phrase "I should" for you. I will allow 3–5 minutes for you to do this.

➤ In the second column, list the advantages of meeting these standards that you have set for yourself. You will have 5 minutes to list these advantages.

➤ In the third column, list the disadvantages of imposing these standards on yourself. I will allow 5 minutes to complete this column.

3. Ask participants to take turns sharing the most unrealistic of their expectations with the group. Encourage the group to brainstorm ways in which participants can discard the self-defeating messages they are sending themselves.

## Variations

- Allow participants to work in teams of two, each interviewing the other and presenting the other's "Shoulds" to the group.

- At a subsequent session, form groups of two or three participants, and ask each group to suggest specific strategies for treating another group's list of "Shoulds."

# What If

This exercise is identical in process to the previous exercise, **I Should**, but focuses on catastrophic thinking.

## Goals

To provide participants with a simple, straightforward way of identifying, analyzing, and treating their own catastrophic thoughts.

To reinforce each participant's sense that it is possible for them to think about anxiety in new ways.

## Group Size

6–12.

## Time

1–2 hours.

## Materials

Pencils; paper.

## Participant Preparation

Pages 59–66 of *Overcoming Panic, Anxiety, & Phobias* will help participants prepare for this session and will reinforce what they learn during the session.

## Process

1. Introduce the exercise by making the following points about catastrophizing:

   ■ People with anxiety problems often dwell on catastrophic thoughts, always anticipating the worst possible consequences.

   ■ You may be a catastrophic thinker without realizing it. You may have worried so long about potential disasters that you no longer recognize that the outcomes you fear are extremely unlikely to happen.

- It is essential for you to subject your catastrophic thoughts to rational analysis. You can't hide from your fears, run away from them, or bury them. The only way you can get rid of them is to examine them carefully.

2. Distribute paper and pencils and give the following directions:

   ➤ With vertical lines, divide your paper into three columns.

   ➤ Write the words "What if" at the top of the first column.

   ➤ In the first column, list your worries, completing the phrase "What if." I will give you 3–5 minutes to complete this column.

   ➤ In the second column, record the catastrophic consequences that you fear may follow the "What ifs." I will allow 5 minutes to do this.

   ➤ In the third column, estimate the likelihood of those catastrophic consequences actually happening. I will give you 3 minutes to complete this column.

3. Ask participants to take turns sharing the most unrealistic of their catastrophic consequences with the group. Encourage the group to brainstorm ways in which participants can discard the self-defeating messages they are sending themselves.

## Variations

- Allow participants to work in teams of two, each interviewing the other and presenting the other's "What ifs" to the group.

- At a subsequent session, form groups of two to three and ask each group to suggest specific strategies for treating another group's list of "What ifs."

# Affirmations for Anxiety Reduction

In this affirmation exercise, participants compile a list of reassuring statements and practice patience by role-playing being supportive to someone with an anxiety problem.

## Goals

To promote patience by practicing it.

To generate for future use a collection of affirmations tied to specific thoughts and events that trigger anxiety.

## Group Size

Unlimited.

## Time

15 minutes.

## Materials

Pencils; paper; easel and easel paper; markers.

## Participant Preparation

Pages 66–74 of *Overcoming Panic, Anxiety, & Phobias* will help participants prepare for this session and will reinforce what they learn during the session.

## Process

1. Introduce the exercise with the following comments:

   ▪ Most people are far more patient with others than they are with themselves.

   ▪ You need to remember that change is difficult and takes time.

   ▪ If you anticipate immediate results, you may become discouraged. If you expect perfection from yourself, you will perpetuate feelings of failure.

- Patience will be a virtue on your road to recovery.

- Today, you'll have the opportunity to practice patience with yourself by pretending to be someone else reacting to your behavior.

2. Distribute paper and pencils. Form groups of four to six participants and provide the following instructions:

   ➤ In your small groups, take turns listing the things that make each of you especially anxious.

   As each person speaks, other members of the group should listen carefully and then respond with soothing, supportive affirmations.

   ➤ Record on paper the affirmations that were given to each of you.

   ➤ Role-play an anxiety-producing situation, using these encouraging words to provide support.

   ➤ You will have about 10 minutes for this activity.

3. Reconvene the entire group. Ask the participants to share the affirmations they received and record them on easel paper.

4. Encourage participants to review the list on the easel paper and to add the most helpful affirmations to their personal list. Suggest that during the next week they attempt to add to their list by thinking of more affirmations, by soliciting suggestions from others, or by collecting them from books.

## Variations

- Group members can compare notes on their encouraging words.

- Suggest that participants can do this exercise at home with close friends and family members.

# Lifestyle Changes

A basic exercise in self-awareness, this procedure helps participants imagine alternatives to what, for too long, has seemed a lifestyle dictated, rather than chosen.

## Goals

To encourage each participant to look objectively at lifestyle issues.

To reinforce each participant's creative participation in objective fact-finding.

## Group Size

6–12.

## Time

1 hour minimum; may be repeated.

## Materials

Pencils; paper; easel and easel paper; markers.

## Process

1. Introduce the negative effects of anxiety on lifestyle with the following comments. Summarize your comments on the easel paper so participants can refer to them.

   ■ You may have difficulty exercising if you fear being outdoors or if you are extremely self-conscious about your body or if the body sensations that occur during vigorous exercise frighten you.

   ■ You may eat poorly if anxiety affects your digestive system or if you fear entering crowded supermarkets or if crowded restaurants bother you and you therefore turn to the high fat foods that are commonly available at drive-ins.

- You may find that addictive substances such as alcohol and prescription drugs are tempting ways to deal with anxiety.

- Supportive relationships may deteriorate if anxiety makes it difficult for you to enter social situations.

2. Comment on the positive effects that lifestyle changes can have on anxiety.

- Vigorous exercise can accustom you to a more rapid heartbeat and make you more tolerant of changes in body sensations. Exercise also produces chemicals in the brain that encourage positive, upbeat feelings.

- Better nutrition will give you the stamina you need to continue on your journey toward recovery.

- If you are overusing alcohol or drugs, reducing your intake of these substances will make you more alert and better able to rationally analyze your anxious thoughts.

3. Distribute paper and pens to participants and provide the following instructions:

➤ Divide your paper into four quadrants.

➤ Label the quadrants with the words exercise, nutrition, relationships, and alcohol and drugs.

➤ In each quadrant, describe your current habits and note any concerns you have about that aspect of your life.

4. When participants appear to have completed their lists, ask them to share any insights they gained, listing common concerns on the easel paper.

5. Take a few minutes to brainstorm concrete steps that participants can take to address their concerns and improve their lifestyles.

6. Conclude the session by restating the importance of good health habits and by encouraging participants, during the next week, to implement one step toward a more healthy lifestyle.

**Variations**

- Allow participants, working in teams, to propose action plans (specific steps, in ascending order of difficulty) that would promote the lifestyle changes desired by each participant.

- Ask participants to list on paper their desired lifestyle changes. Collect and distribute these papers to other group members. Then have participants develop an action plan for the person whose paper they have received. Redistribute the action plans and ask participants to comment on the action plan that was recommended for them.

# Can-Do: My Targets for Personal Change

Participants fill out a worksheet that helps them focus on achievable goals.

## Goals

To promote thoughts about change.

To assess the impact of anxiety on the ability to alter lifestyles.

To develop some strategies to start lifestyle changes and to gain information on what this change process is like.

## Group Size

Unlimited.

## Time

1–3 hours.

## Materials

Pencils; easel and easel paper; markers; **I Can Do It** worksheet.

## Process

1. Introduce the tension between the desire for dramatic change and the need to set achievable goals by making the following comments:

   ▪ I would love to be rich—to inherit a million dollars, to win 10 million in the lottery. Chances of this happening are pretty remote, so I should probably set my sights on a more achievable goal such as establishing a plan that will ensure financial security after retirement.

   ▪ As you work towards recovery from anxiety and panic, you may be imaging dramatic changes in your lifestyle, ones that will bring fame, fortune, and unending happiness.

   ▪ Don't stop yourself from imagining these changes. It's encouraging to think about all the possibilities that life may hold for you.

■ It's important, however, to set some achievable goals—steps on the road toward major lifestyle changes. These targets for change should be "can-dos," goals that you can, with effort, successfully implement.

■ Your success at achieving one goal will make it possible for you to attempt the next on your list. Whereas your failure to make a dramatic change in your life would only discourage you and make it harder for you to keep trying.

2. Distribute the **I Can Do It** worksheet and provide the following instructions, giving time after each instruction for participants to write:

➤ In the left column of your worksheet, list the changes you would like to see in your life. Let your imagination run wild as you suggest dramatic, sweeping changes.

➤ In the right column, suggest one realistic step towards implementing, in some way, each of the exciting changes that you have listed.

➤ Select one of the steps that you listed, the easiest to implement, and record it in the section headed "First step."

➤ Next, think about how your anxiety problem may affect your attempts to implement this lifestyle change. Record any problems that you anticipate in the section headed "Stumbling blocks."

3. Reassemble the group and give the following instructions:

➤ One at a time, I'd like you to report on the specific change you would like to make and the potential stumbling blocks that concern you.

➤ After each participant speaks, the other members of the group will suggest ways that the stumbling block might be eliminated.

➤ Record their suggestions, along with your own ideas, in "Solutions," the final section of your worksheet.

4. Encourage participants to take their first step during the following week. Tell them that you will ask for reports on their progress at the group's next meeting.

☞ *When you ask for reports, be sure to offer lots of praise for any effort that they make toward reaching their goals.*

## I CAN DO IT

| Dramatic exciting changes | Realistic first steps |
|---|---|
|  |  |

**First step**

**Stumbling blocks**

**Solutions**

# Looking at My Defenses

The following exercise will help participants sort out the differences between defenses that work and those that don't. The session should be led by a mental health professional.

## Goals

To allow participants to look at their defenses.

To help participants evaluate which defenses are working and which are not.

## Group Size

6–10.

## Time

1 hour minimum; may be repeated.

## Materials

Pencils; paper; easel and easel paper; markers.

## Process

1. Introduce the session by making the following comments about defense mechanisms:

   ■ Everyone develops defenses to keep them safe, and many of these defenses are essential to our physical, mental, and emotional health.

   ■ If you avoid walking along dark streets in unfamiliar areas of town, you will be less likely to be mugged than if you are careless about your physical safety.

   ■ If you always wear a seat belt, you are exercising appropriate caution that may prevent injuries in case of an accident.

   ■ If you refuse to be troubled or insulted by careless comments from coworkers, you are protecting your emotional health.

- At times, however, the ways in which you try to protect yourself are part of your problem.

- If you ensure your physical safety by never going out after dark or by refusing to drive at all, your defenses are restricting your freedom.

- If you protect yourself from being hurt by other people by refusing to socialize, you are eliminating the pleasure that relationships bring.

- If you try to protect your children from the dangers of life by smothering them with rules and restrictions, your defenses are actually injuring them.

- It can be frightening to eliminate defenses that have seemed essential. After you identify some of your defenses, you will have the opportunity to take an easy first step by imagining yourself living without one of them.

2. Distribute paper and pencils and ask participants to list the defenses they have set up to deal with their anxiety. If they have difficulty with this process, be ready to help with questions or more examples.

3. When all participants appear to have listed one or more items, introduce the visualization that follows by asking participants to select from their list a defense mechanism that is not serving them well, one they would like to eliminate. Then read the script slowly, pausing to allow people to fully imagine each scene.

   *Sit back in your chair and get comfortable. Slowly, take a deep breath . . . and exhale. Again, inhale . . . and exhale. As you continue to breathe slowly and comfortably, imagine yourself using the defense that you have now decided is not helpful. Develop the scene as fully as possible. Let yourself imagine the benefits of this defense . . . how safe it makes you feel.*

   *Now begin to imagine the disadvantages of using this defense. Imagine yourself feeling oppressed by the way it is affecting your life. Let yourself feel the weight of it, as you develop the scene fully in your mind.*

©1996 Whole Person Press 210 W Michigan Duluth MN 55802      (800) 247-6789

*Inhale . . . and exhale. Continue to breathe slowly and gently as you begin to imagine your life without this defense . . . the freedom you will have when you discard ways of thinking and acting that no longer serve you well. Imagine yourself in a situation that would cause you to use this defense . . . how will you feel without it? If you have any feelings of anxiety, focus on your slow, deep breathing.*

*Now imagine yourself feeling light and free as you discard this now useless way of thinking and acting . . . allow yourself to fully imagine the joyful freedom you will have in your thoughts and activities and relationships.*

*When you are ready, slowly open your eyes and look around.*

4. Conclude the session with the following comments:

   ▪ I encourage you to take time this week to imagine yourself without this defense mechanism.

   ▪ As it becomes easier and more comfortable to imagine yourself without it, you will become ready to enter an anxiety-producing situation without resorting to its use. Try that in real life.

   ▪ Go on to imagine yourself discarding another defense that you no longer need. Continue this process, beginning with the easier defenses and continuing with those that appear more difficult.

   ▪ The confidence that you will gain as you eliminate one defense mechanism after another will encourage you to continue.

## Variation

   ▪ Allow participants to work in teams, role-playing the elimination of one or two defenses as described by individual members of the group. Each role-playing episode should be followed by convening the entire group for a brief discussion during which each defense is described along with what it would be like to live without it.

# Wish List

This exercise introduces participants to their own imaginative reconstruction.

## Goals

To allow participants to act out their own best images of themselves.

To reinforce participants' creative participation in finding solutions to their problems.

## Group Size

6–12.

## Time

1–1/2 hour minimum.

## Materials

Pencils; paper.

## Process

1. Introduce the exercise with the following comments:

   ▪ Everyone imagines being someone else from time to time.

   ▪ Imagining being someone else can be an important first step in actually giving yourself more options, more satisfaction and pleasure, which is, after all, why you came to this group in the first place!

   ▪ You may imagine yourself living a very different life than you do now, or perhaps you imagine yourself leading much the same life but without the constraints placed on you by anxiety and fear of panic episodes.

2. Distribute paper and pencils to participants and provide the following instructions:

➤ On this paper, write a short script between you, as you would like yourself to be, and a friend, coworker, or social acquaintance. In this script, show yourself at your imaginary best—bright, competent, comfortable, fluent, perhaps even witty.

➤ You will have 10 minutes to develop this two-person script.

3. Introduce the role-playing aspect of this activity with the following instructions:

➤ Select a partner to role-play your script with you.

➤ One at a time, partners will act out their scripts.

➤ After each role play is complete, we'll pause for the actors and the audience to comment on what they saw.

4. Conclude the session with supportive comments about the courage participants showed in revealing their imaginary selves. Encourage them to keep the image of that self in front of them as they continue on the road to recovery.

## Variation

■ Allow participants to simply write their scripts without actually staging them.

# Resources

# Writing Treatment Plans and Measuring Outcomes

### Cognitive-behavior therapy

Cognitive-behavior therapy has demonstrated effectiveness for treating a variety of emotional problems, including anxiety disorders. Cognitive-behavior therapy is an effective, brief therapy which emphasizes awareness of the interconnection of thoughts, emotions (such as anxiety), and behavior. It is a skill-based therapy which primarily focuses on the "here and now," and encourages a collaborative, problem-focused approach between therapist and client. Homework is assigned so that the client becomes aware of how their thoughts and actions might be contributing to their distress. Homework also facilitates learning of new skills which are then applied in daily life to promote change. Maintenance of gains and relapse prevention are viewed as essential components of treatment. Assessment of life stressors, social environment, underlying dysfunctional beliefs from childhood as well as biological factors are all viewed as important factors to consider in the change process.

### Biopsychosocial assessment

A thorough biopyschosocial assessment of clients provides the foundation for accurate diagnoses, treatment goals, collaboration with other health providers, and evaluation of clients' progress. Although this process has always been important, currently it is even more essential. Managed care organizations audit their providers' case records as part of their own quality improvement efforts and in order to meet national quality review standards for accreditation. If you want to be in provider networks, you will need to be in compliance with these standards.

The following data must appear in all charts: identifying information including the client's name, address, phone number, employer, and primary care doctor; assessment/intake information including the precipitating event, problem areas and symptoms, mental status exam, alcohol and substance abuse screening, associated family, social work history, suicidal ideation/intent, any threats of violence (homicidal ideation), health problems and risks, previous mental health usage, and diagnoses on all five DSM axes.

The treatment plan, including specific target goals, interventions, and outcome measures, should be based on current symptoms that are creating problems in functioning (thereby demonstrating medical necessity) and that are related directly to the DSM Axis I diagnoses. The rationale for referral to other health providers, including a medication evaluation, should be clearly stated. Target goals need to be specific and progress behaviorally observable. Suggested time frames for treatment should be in keeping with the most efficient, currently approved modalities for returning clients to their previous level of functioning. In the case of anxiety disorders, cognitive-behavior therapy, psychotropic medication, or a combination of both are recommended. These treatment interventions have been validated through research and are continually being modified as a result of new research projects.

Progress notes, which should be problem focused, must be signed and dated. Collaboration with other health providers should be noted and discharge summaries completed.

Each client's treatment plan should be designed, whenever possible, in collaboration with the client. The therapist and client need to clearly understand the target goals of treatment, the amount of time anticipated, and the specific strategies that will be employed. The treatment plan is reassessed with the client and modified as needed to achieve the target goals. The client should be given homework assignments and strategies which they can continue to use on their own after formal treatment is complete. Relapse prevention is an integral part of treatment for maintenance of gains.

On the following pages, you will find tips on how to write appropriate treatment plans and goals for anxiety disorders along with some simple outcome scales with which you can document clients' progress. Every managed care organization is collecting outcome data and you will be in the vanguard if you can demonstrate that you are collecting measures on your own. You will also gain information you can analyze and use to update your treatment techniques.

Keep in mind the following list of characteristics when you write treatment plans. They should:

- Be goal oriented
- Be client negotiated
- Provide both  pretreatment assessment and measurement
- Be well suited for brief, problem-focused treatment
- Increase the client's motivation for change thus enhancing the therapeutic alliance
- Include an estimated termination date
- Provide ways to demonstrate clinical effectiveness for client, therapists, managed care organizations, and other referral sources

## How to define treatment goals

### 1. Elicit a list of goals.

Ask the client "If you accomplish what you hope to during this therapy, in what ways will you and your life be changed?" Or, ask the client, "In four weeks how will you know that this therapy has helped? What changes will you need to see in order to know you're on the right track?" Use their answers to help write their goals.

### 2. Reframe goals, developing positive statements from negative ones.

"I'll stop my panic in the grocery line," becomes "I'll remain calm when in a grocery line."

"I won't people-please," becomes "I'll increase my assertiveness."

" I'll never be worried," becomes "I'll challenge excess worry about my health with actual evidence."

### 3. Make each goal as specific as possible, using one or more concrete examples.

Ask the client "What will be different when you have achieved this goal? How will we know that you've accomplished it?"

If, for example, a client's goal is to challenge excessive worry about his or her health, the specific behavioral definitions might include those listed below:

■ I'll keep focused on my doctor's report that my health is good.

■ I'll join a fitness club. I'll read chapter 6 in *Overcoming Panic, Anxiety, & Phobias* to learn how to expose myself to my rapid heartbeat.

■ I'll resist the urge to check for reassurance from my husband when I worry about a heart attack. I'll allow myself to experience hyperventilation, breathe slowly, and challenge my catastrophic thoughts.

## Sample treatment plan

Develop a treatment plan form similar to the one illustrated below. Complete the plan during your assessment session, designing it in collaboration with your client. In column titled "end date" record the date you expect the client to reach the goal. Use the information on this form along with pertinent assessment data to write your managed care report, to communicate with other health providers, and to focus treatment interventions in upcoming therapy sessions.

---

**Treatment Plan**

Client _____ Date _____

DSM Diagnoses _____

Problem(s) _____

| Goals | Measures | Interventions | End-Date |
|-------|----------|---------------|----------|
| 1. _____ | _____ | _____ | _____ |
| 2. _____ | _____ | _____ | _____ |
| 3. _____ | _____ | _____ | _____ |
| 4. _____ | _____ | _____ | _____ |
| 5. _____ | _____ | _____ | _____ |
| 6. _____ | _____ | _____ | _____ |

---

## Demonstrating your treatment results

Currently, providers are being asked to document the clinical effectiveness of their treatment for managed care organizations (MCO). Although using outcome measurements may be unfamiliar to you at this time, there are many fairly easy ways to build this process into your treatment plan. As a result, you will be able to substantiate the clinical effectiveness of your treatment to yourself and to managed care organizations. In addition, you will have gathered data for reassessing your particular treatment strategies and altering them as needed.

## Characteristics of outcome measurements

Outcome measurements should be:

- Practice driven
- Flexible
- Able to quantify changes that take place during the entire treatment process, beginning with pretreatment assessment and concluding with discharge
- Designed to enable the clinician to meet increasing demands for accountability
- A facilitator for enhanced communication with managed care reviewers
- A vehicle to provide clinicians and patients with feedback about treatment interventions

## How to measure change

You can develop your own subjective, nonvalidated rating scales. However, you may wish to use some of the measurement tools that have been developed by other therapists. You will want to have scales available to measure intensity, frequency, duration, and progress. The brief list provided below will give you a place to start.

1. Anxiety rating scale

| 0 | 1 | 2 | 3 | 4 | 5 | 6 | 7 | 8 | 9 | 10 |
|---|---|---|---|---|---|---|---|---|---|----|

   no anxiety                                    extreme anxiety

2. Likert scales

| 1 | 2 | 3 | 4 | 5 | 6 | 7 |
|---|---|---|---|---|---|---|
| not at all | | | | | | completely |

| 1 | 2 | 3 | 4 | 5 | 6 | 7 |
|---|---|---|---|---|---|---|
| never | | | | | | always |

| 1 | 2 | 3 | 4 | 5 | 6 | 7 |
|---|---|---|---|---|---|---|
| none | | | | | | all |

3. GAF Scale (Global Assessment of Functioning) AXIS V DSM

The therapist rates the client's psychological, social, and occupational functioning on a 1–90 scale.

| 1 | 90 |
|---|---|
| severe illness | relative health |

4. Frequency counts: By week, by day, by session
5. The overall percent of time something occurs
6. Modified use of standardized measures (selected items)
7. Behavioral performance (rated by therapist/client)
8. Progress towards completion of goals

| 1% | 100% |
|---|---|
| pretreatment | goal reached |

## Sample treatment plans

On the following pages, you will find sample treatment plans for panic disorder with agoraphobia, generalized anxiety disorder, social phobia, and specific phobia. Each plan includes target goals, interventions, and measurements.

Specific goals and strategies have been designed for each particular case. These strategies do not necessarily represent standard treatment plans for any particular anxiety disorder; however, the basic strategies are ones that, based on research, are currently felt to have merit.

The column titled "end date" should contain the estimated completion date.

## Sample Treatment Plan #1

**Problem(s)** Fear/Worry regarding health and finances

**DSM Diagnoses Axis I**: Generalized anxiety disorder and finances

| Goals | Measure | Intervention | End-Date |
|---|---|---|---|
| 1. Identify and challenge thoughts associated with excess worry. Client will increase use of adaptive, realty-based cognitions regarding illness and finances. | On a scale from 1–10, therapist will rate client on effective use of positive self-statements when appropriate; ratings will begin prior to treatment and will be done bimonthly. | Read *Overcoming Panic, Anxiety, & Phobias*. Fill out cognitive charts—cognitive restructuring after looking at the probability and severity of health and financial concerns. | |
| 2. Increase ability to relax and decrease muscle tension; increase awareness of situations and thoughts which increase muscle tension, and develop the ability to lessen tension on cue; increase the use of exercise as a tension reliever. | Client will record his tension/relaxation ratings five times per week and will engage in three exercise sessions per week. | Provide client with relaxation tapes and charts. Support client in using cue-controlled relaxation and physical exercise as stress releasers. | |
| | Client will rate his anxiety on a scale from 1–10 when imagining worry stimuli. | Exposure in imagination (in session and home practice). Exposure in-vivo to worry hierarchy. | |
| 3. Increase appropriate emotional and physiological reactivity to excess worry regarding illness stimuli, financial disaster, hospital signs, TV news, performance reviews, and paying bills; increase ability to spend realistic sums of money with less fear. | Therapist will rate client's worry and intrusive thinking on a scale from 1 to 10. Client will fill out security moves worksheet to document results of behavioral experiments. | Conduct behavioral experiments—i.e. pay bills without pacing or procrastinating; write budget; spend realistic, planned amount of money for enjoyment; challenge excess worry thoughts. | |
| 4. Identify family of origin factors that encourage worry thoughts and dysfunctional assumptions (i.e. critical father, sister's chronic illness). | Client will self-report his discomfort about these worries and assumptions, rating it on a scale from 1 to 10. | Identification and exploration of themes/issues associated with excess worries/assumptions—referral to self-help group. | |

## Sample Treatment Plan #2

**Problem(s)** Avoids restaurants, parties

**DSM Diagnoses Axis I:** Social phobia

| Goals | Measure | Intervention | End-Date |
|---|---|---|---|
| 1. Increase ability to tolerate anxiety in general and also specific anxieties related to social interactions. | On a scale from 1 to 10, client will self-rate feelings of anxiety and tension. | Progressive muscle relaxation, cue controlled relaxation, meditation. | |
| 2. Participate in an anxiety management group to learn coping skills and gain exposure to feared social situations. | Client will complete ratings on the **Anxiety/Panic Targets for Change** form during the first group meeting. | Read *Overcoming Panic, Anxiety, & Phobias* and then do the homework. Support client's attempts at in-vivo exposure as she tests her ability to participate in group discussions while anxious. | |
| 3. Gain awareness of assumptions contributing to social anxiety and begin to challenge dysfunctional assumptions. | Client will self-rate assumptions regarding perfectionism and control. Pretreatment: List dysfunctional assumptions. | Cognitive restructuring and behavioral experiments. Explore relevant family of origin issues. Assertiveness training. | |
| 4. Reduce behavioral avoidance. Increase ability to enter restaurants and attend social gatherings. | On the anxiety rating scale, client will self-rate anxiety when exposed to social stimuli. Pretreatment: List avoided situations—check each entry as client engages in graded self-exposure. | Exposure in imagination. Construct hierachy of feared social stimuli, sensory exercises, graded self-exposure, relapse prevention. | |

## Sample Treatment Plan #3

**Problem(s)** Test anxiety and avoidance

**DSM Diagnoses Axis I**: Specific phobia

| Goals | Measure | Intervention | End-Date |
|-------|---------|--------------|----------|
| 1. Increase understanding of the three response system (cognitive, physiological, and behavioral) involved in anxiety and test anxiety. | Therapist rating of client knowledge of three response system on a scale from 1 to 5. | Discussion of three response system as it relates to test anxiety. Read *Overcoming Panic, Anxiety, & Phobias*. Fill out forms. | |
| 2. Increase ability to relax in general and also in relationship to sensations of test anxiety. | Self-ratings of anxiety/tension on a scale from 1 to 10. | Progressive deep muscle relaxation and breath retraining. | |
| 3. Increase adaptive cognitions as they relate to test anxiety; identify and challenge thoughts which trigger or maintain anxiety and avoidance. | Therapist ratings of effective use of positive statements on a scale from 1 to 10. | Cognitive restructuring. Fill out forms in *Overcoming Panic, Anxiety, & Phobias* and process in session. | |
| 4. Increase ability to lower physiological reactivity to test anxiety cues. | Self-rating, using the anxiety rating scale, of anxiety when imagining cues. | Graded exposure in imagination; sensory exercises; role play test taking. | |
| 5. Confront behavioral avoidance to test stimuli with exposure and maintenance of nonreactivity to test fear cues. | Self-rating, using the anxiety rating scale, of anxiety when exposed to test stimuli. | Enroll in class for in-vivo exposure; relapse prevention. | |

## Sample Treatment Plan #4

**Problem(s)** Panic attacks, avoidance of stores freeways

**DSM Diagnoses Axis I**: Panic disorder with agoraphobia

| Goals | Measure | Intervention | End-Date |
|---|---|---|---|
| 1. Increase understanding of panic and identify specific cues which trigger panic attacks and avoidance. | Panic and anxiety response form Pretreatment: Therapist rating of client knowledge about panic/avoidance on a scale from 1 to 5. | Read *Overcoming Panic, Anxiety, & Phobias*. Discuss specific anxiety triggers, thoughts, physical sensations, behavior, anxiety rating in group. | |
| 2. Challenge thoughts that trigger and intensify panic attacks. | Therapist rating of adaptive cognitions and positive self-statements on a scale from 1 to 5. | Read sections in book on catastrophic thinking. Fill out forms and discuss in group. | |
| 3. Attain methods to reduce psychomotor symptoms of panic. | Self-rating of anxiety and tension on a scale from 1 to 10. | Practice meditation, mini-meditations during stress, breath retraining. Cue controlled relaxation. | |
| 4. Lower anxiety and worry about feared physical sensations and situations. | Self-ratings of anxious apprehension on a scale from 1 to 10. | Use strategies regarding worry/anticipatory anxiety during the week. Problem solve with groups —exposure in imagination practice. | |
| 5. Increase ability to assert self at work and in family situations and to label emotions other than anxiety. | Self-report of assertiveness on a scale from 1 to 10. | Assertiveness training; behavioral rehearsal; conjoint therapy session with husband. Referral to couples communication class. | |
| 6. Increase tolerance. Client will enter with 80% less fear of all situations currently avoided or entered only when accompanied by family members. | Complete checklist of exposure to feared situations and physical sensations pre- and posttreatment Frequency and intensity of panic attacks and avoidance. | Read exposure chapter in *Overcoming Panic, Anxiety, & Phobias*; exposure list, graded exposure to stores, freeways; problems solve PRN; Sensory Exercises (interoceptive cueing); relapse prevention. | |

# Bibliography

American Psychiatric Association. *Diagnostic and Statistical Manual of Mental Disorders.* (4th ed.) Washington, D.C., 1994.

Barlow, D.H. *Anxiety and Its Disorders: The Nature and Treatment of Anxiety and Panic.* New York: Guilford Press, 1988.

Barlow, D.H. *Clinical Handbook of Psychological Disorders* (2nd ed.) (ch. 1, p. 1–47); (ch. 3, p. 99–136); (ch. 4, p. 137–188). New York: International Universities Press, 1993.

Barlow, D.H. "Cognitive-behavioral Approaches to Panic Disorder and Social Phobia." *Bull. Menninger Clin.* 56 (2, suppl A): A14–A28, 1992.

Barlow, D.H. "The Nature of Anxiety: Anxiety, Depression, and Emotional Disorders." In R.M. Rapee & D.H. Barlow (eds.), *Chronic anxiety: Generalized anxiety disorder and mixed anxiety-depression* (pp. 1–28) New York: Guilford Press.

Barr Taylor, C., and B. Arnow. *The Nature and Treatment of Anxiety Disorders,* New York: International Universities Press, 1988.

Beck, A.T., G. Emery and R. Greenberg. *Anxiety Disorders and Phobias: A Cognitive Perspective.* New York; Guilford Press, 1985.

Beck, J.S. *Cognitive Therapy: Basics and Beyond.* New York: Guilford, 1994.

Burns, S.D. *Feeling Good: The New Mood Therapy.* New York: William Morrow & Company, 1980.

Clark, D.M., ed. "Special Issue: Panic Disorders." *J Cognitive Psychotherapy.* 5:3, Fall 1991.

Cox, B.J., et al. "Suicidal Ideation and Suicide Attempts in Panic Disorder and Social Phobia." *Am J Psychiatry.* 151(6):882–887, 1994.

Craske, M., R. Bunt, R.M. Rapee, and D.H. Barlow. "Perceived control and controllability during in vivo exposure: Spider phobics." *Journal of Anxiety Disorders.* 5: 285–292, 1991.

DiNardo, P.A., I and D.H. Barlow. *Anxiety Disorders Interview Schedule Revised, (ADIS-R).* Albany, New York: Phobia and Anxiety Disorders Clinic, State University of New York at Albany, 1988.